THE LIFE

OF

JOHN KNOX,

THE SCOTTISH REFORMER.

WRITTEN FOR THE AMERICAN SUNDAY-SCHOOL UNION, AND
REVISED BY THE COMMITTEE OF PUBLICATION.

PHILADELPHIA:

AMERICAN SUNDAY-SCHOOL UNION
NO. 146 CHESTNUT STREET.

First printing: January 2011

For information write:
New Leaf Publishing Group, P.O. Box 726, Green Forest, AR 72638.
Attic Books is a division of the New Leaf Publishing Group, Inc.

ISBN-13: 978-0-89051-602-7

Library of Congress Number: 2010915577

Printed in the United States of America

Please visit our website for other great titles: www.nlpg.com

Originally published in 1833 by:

American Sunday-School Union

Now known as:

American Missionary Fellowship

www.americanmissionary.org

ENTERED according to the Act of Congress, in the year 1833, by PAUL BECK, Jr. Treasurer, in trust for the American Sunday-school Union, in the Clerk's Office of the District Court of the Eastern District of Pennsylvania.

CONTENTS.

INTRODUCTION.

CHAPTER I.

CHAPTER II.

CHAPTER III.

CHAPTER IV.

CHAPTER V.

6   CONTENTS.

CHAPTER X.

CHAPTER XI.

CHAPTER XII.

CHAPTER XIII.

PUBLISHER'S NOTE

The ASSU, now called American Missionary Fellowship (AMF), has been associated with some of America's most prominent citizens and religious leaders. Included among ASSU officers or influenced by its mission were Bishop William White of Philadelphia's Christ Church; Bushrod Washington (President George Washington's nephew); Francis Scott Key, who wrote "The Star Spangled Banner"; D.L. Moody; Laura Ingalls Wilder; and John Adams (related to both early American presidents), who personally organized over 320 Sunday schools.

ASSU missionaries carried books published by the mission in saddlebags to leave with the fledgling Sunday schools they had started, promoting literacy, education, and the very best in Christian moral values. Though it stopped publishing books in 1968, American Missionary Fellowship continues its missionary work in the United States, extending beyond Sunday school work to include church planting, church camps, and numerous other programs.

http://www.americanmissionary.org/

INTRODUCTION.

Preliminary remarks on the religious condition of Scotland, from the third century, the date of the introduction of the gospel into Scotland, down to the time of John Knox, the great Scotch Reformer.

As early as the third century of the Christian era, Scotland appears to have been blessed with the light of the gospel ; and the persecution under the Roman emperor Dioclesian, in the beginning of the fourth century, compelled many Christians, among whom were several preachers, to repair to that country, where they diligently laboured to extirpate idolatry, and establish Christianity. From the retired life of these emigrants, and their devotedness to the service of God, they were called Culdees.

In the fifth century, however, the pope of Rome, who had already enslaved the greater part of Europe, cast his eye on

Scotland, and began to employ means for bringing it also under the papal yoke. He accordingly sent a person of considerable learning, named Palladius, from Rome, for the purpose of confuting the heresies of Pelagius, which had begun to spread over the country. By degrees, popery came to be universally acknowledged ; and in a few centuries afterwards, it was firmly established throughout the kingdom.

During this period, several eminent servants of Christ fearlessly opposed the super stitions and idolatries of the Romish religion. Among others, two Culdees, in the seventh century, named Clemens and Samson, rejected the usurped power of the papal see, and maintained that Christ alone was the head of the Christian church. But such lights as these proved quite insufficient to dispel that moral darkness which had enveloped the church ; and although it was about the fourteenth century before the Culdees were extinct, it was not till the beginning of the fifteenth, that the light of the reformation began to dawn.

About 1407, John Resby, a scholar of John Wickliffe of England (one of the pope's great opponents), came to Scotland. Imitating his master, he declaimed against the errors of the Romish church, and boldly preached the gospel wherever an opportunity was afforded. But in a short time the emissaries of Rome condemned him to the flames. About ten years afterwards, Paul Craw, a follower of John Huss, the Bohemian reformer, suffered the same fate. In 1528, Patrick Hamilton, an eminent martyr, was likewise condemned in the twenty-fourth year of his age, and sealed his testimony with his blood in the city of St. Andrews ; and from this period, till the burning of Walter Mill, the church of Rome was upheld in Scotland solely by means of fire and sword. Multitudes then fell victims to the tyranny of that church, which has in all ages " shed the blood of the saints."

Among this number was the famous George Wishart, who also perished in the flames at St. Andrews, in 1546.* The martyrdom of Walter Mill, however, in 1568, gave the death—blow to popery in Scotland ; but as these transactions occurred during the life of Knox, reference will again be made to them in the course of the ensuing biography.

The enemies of the truth triumphed long in Scotland ; and liberty, either civil or religious, was so little understood before the reformation, that whatever was the will of the Catholic priests, was received by the people with the most superstitious reverence. The corruption of the clergy was extreme ; ignorance, idleness, dissipation, and pride, armed with power, were the characteristics of these spiritual guides. They made no attempts to secure the affections of the people ; but ruled both over the souls and bodies of men, with a tyran-

* The Life of Wishart is published by the American Sunday-school Union.

ny which appears at this day to be hardly credible.

" The form of popery which prevailed in Scotland," says Dr. Robertson, " was of the most bigoted and illiberal kind. Those doctrines which are most apt to shock the human understanding, and those legends which farthest exceed belief, were proposed to the people without any attempt to palliate or disguise them ; nor did they ever call in question the reasonableness of the one, or the truth of the other. The nature of the functions of the popish clergy gave them access to all persons, and at all seasons. They haunted the weak and credulous ; they besieged the beds of the sick and of the dying ; they suffered few to go out of the world, without leaving marks of their liberality to the church, and taught them *to compound with the Almighty for their sins, by bestowing riches on those who called themselves his servants.*"*

* History of Scotland, Book II.

But the seeds of divine truth had been scattered among the hitherto superstitious and ignorant multitude by a few sincere and faithful servants of Christ; and in spite of all opposition, in a few years spread over the nation at large. Every effort, indeed, which either force or fraud could invent, was made by the supporters of the church of Rome, to prevent the downfall of their idolatrous establishment. But He who works, and none can hinder it, raised up instruments fitted for accomplishing all his purposes of mercy; and among these none was so conspicuous for his burning zeal, and unbending faithfulness, as John Knox, who has been emphatically called the reformer of Scotland.

LIFE OF JOHN KNOX

CHAPTER I.

Birth of Knox—Is educated at the same time with the celebrated historian, George Buchanan—Buchanan becomes
a literary man—Knox turns all his attention to theology
—Imbibes the doctrines of the Reformation—Repairs to
East Lothian, where he is appointed tutor in the Douglas
family—Attends the sermons of Thomas Guilliam, and
becomes fully convinced of the errors of Popery.

JOHN KNOX was born in the year 1505,
at Gifford, near Haddington, in East Lothian, Scotland, and was descended from
an ancient and honourable family.   Although his parents were not in affluent
circumstances, they were able at least to
give him a liberal education.   Accordingly he was first sent to the grammar
school at Haddington, where he studied
the Latin language.   He was afterwards
removed to the university of Glasgow,
where, with George Buchanan, the celebrated historian, he was placed under the
tuition of Mr. John Mair or Major, who
at that time was professor of theology

and philosophy. Mair appears to have entertained juster sentiments regarding the power of the church than was common in that age. He denied the power of the pope to consecrate or dethrone kings ; and maintained that his excommunications could have no force if unjustly pronounced. He censured the avarice and pride of the court of Rome, and wished the abolition of holydays, and the suppression of monasteries. Such sentiments as these both Knox and Buchanan afterwards boldly defended. The instructions of Mair, however, which were in general of a trifling and superstitious description, soon disgusted these two scholars, and they began to employ themselves in quite different studies. While Buchanan turned his attention to literature and poetry, Knox employed his time in searching after divine truth. He continued, however, to attend the instructions of Mair, and soon became so remarkable for his knowledge of the theology of that age, that he obtained the degree of Master of Arts while very young. Having directed his attention to divinity, he was also ordained before the usual time allotted by the rules of the church.

While engaged in these studies, the

doctrines of the reformation, which were spreading over the country, led him diligently to inquire into the tenets and practice of the church of Rome. In searching into the writings of the ancient fathers, especially the works of Jerome and Augustin, he plainly perceived how different their doctrines were from those to which he had been accustomed. The continual references to Scripture also in which they abounded, led him to the perusal of the sacred volume, where alone can be learned " the truth as it is in Jesus." Accordingly, about 1635, he quitted the study of scholastic theology, and applied himself to a plainer, and more simple system of divinity ; and although it was about seven years after this before he openly professed the protestant religion, God, in mercy, not to him only, but to the nation at large, gradually enlightened his mind to perceive the difference between the pure doctrines of his holy word, and the vain and absurd traditions of men.

A favourable opinion of the reformed religion being discovered in his lectures, Knox was obliged to repair, in 1542, to East Lothian, where he was appointed tutor to the distinguished families of

Douglas and Cockburn, who favoured the reformation. While residing there, he enjoyed the opportunity of attending the sermons of a friar, named Thomas Guilliam, who was one of the chaplains of the earl of Arran, at that time regent of Scotland, and a bold defender of the protestant doctrines. It was under the ministry of this man that Knox was led to a better acquaintance with evangelical truth, and became fully convinced of the errors of popery.

CHAPTER II.

The Earl of Arran appointed Regent of Scotland—Promotes the reading of the Bible in English, which had been deemed heresy—The Regent obliged by Cardinal Beaton, Archbishop of St. Andrew's, to renounce the doctrine of the Reformers—Character, persecution, and murder of George Wishart—Cardinal Beaton assassinated for his tyranny—The conspirators take refuge in the castle of St. Andrew's, which they defend—Knox, persecuted for the doctrines he taught, is obliged to take refuge in the castle—Continues to lecture in the castle—The solemn and remarkable manner in which Knox was called to the office of Reformer—Great change takes place in him—His first sermon directed against the antichristian nature of the church of Rome—Efforts made to cause Knox and other leaders to abjure what the papists denominated *heresy*—The preaching of the Reformer eminently successful.

THE earl of Arran was appointed regent in 1542, on the death of James the Fifth. At first he professed the greatest attachment to the reformed opinions, and not only chose two protestant preachers to be his chaplains, but in his first parliament an act was passed allowing "every man who could read to use the English translation of the Bible, until the prelates should publish another more correct." This act proved of immense advantage to the cause of the reformation. Formerly the reading of the sacred Scriptures had been declared heresy; but the privilege which all now enjoyed, of perusing the book of God, opened the eyes of multitudes. The writings of several foreign protestants, which were at this time dispersed over the country, aided in exposing the absurdities and antichristian nature of popery. The regent, however, was afraid of exciting the aversion of the Roman catholics; and cardinal Beaton, archbishop of St. Andrew's, using every artifice to change the regent's sentiments, at length succeeded in bringing him publicly to renounce the doctrine of the reformers. The cardinal, having gained this much, immediately exerted all his influence in persecuting the opposers of the Romish church. The reading of the Bible was prohibited, and many were dragged to tortures and to

death for their adherence to the testimony
of Christ.

During this persecution, George Wishart,
who had been banished for teaching the
Greek Testament, returned to Scotland in
1544, and immediately began to preach
the gospel. Wishart was a most amiable and interesting man. Learned and
eloquent, irreproachable in life, and courteous and affable in manners ; his fervent
piety was tempered by uncommon meek-
ness, patience, prudence, and charity.
Multitudes flocked to hear him ; and Knox
himself was so charmed with his doctrines
and eloquence, that he became a constant
attendant. It was about two years after
his return to Scotland, during which time
he had laboured night and day for the
spiritual good of his countrymen, that this
excellent man was apprehended by the
earl of Bothwell at Ormiston. He had
come from Haddington that night, after
preaching a farewell sermon, as if pre-
dicting his martyrdom ; and though Knox
insisted on accompanying him to Ormiston,
he would not suffer him, but dismissed
him with these words : " Nay, return to
your children (meaning his scholars), and
God bless you ; one is sufficient for a

sacrifice." Wishart was delivered over to
cardinal Beaton, and in a convocation of
bishops and clergy was condemned to the
flames! How dreadful were the sufferings
of Christians in former times, and how
meekly and patiently did they endure even
unto death, rather than renounce or betray
the truth!

The murder of Wishart excited an almost universal indignation against Beaton,
and Norman Leslie, the eldest son of the
earl of Rothes, who had received many
private injuries from the cardinal, resolved
with a few others to take the life of that
tyrant. This resolution ought most severely to be condemned; for however
wicked that individual might have been,
his assassination can admit of no excuse.
"The cardinal at that time," says Dr.
Robertson, "resided in the castle of St.
Andrew's, (situated on a rocky eminence
overlooking the sea,) which he had fortified at great expense, and in the opinion of
the age had rendered impregnable. His
retinue was numerous, the town at his de-
votion, and the neighbouring country full
of his dependants. In this situation, six-
teen persons undertook to surprise his
castle, and to assassinate himself; and

their success was equal to the boldness of the attempt.   Early in the morning (May 29, 1546) they seized on the gate of the castle, which was set open to the workmen who were employed in finishing the fortification ; and having placed sentries at the door of the cardinal's apartment, they awakened his numerous domestics one by one, and turning them out of the castle, they, without noise, or tumult, or violence to any other person, delivered their country."*

Conscious that their crime exposed them to punishment, they fortified the castle, and managed to hold out against the regent for five months.   A truce was at length concluded, by which the conspirators were to receive a pardon, if they would surrender the castle.   Neither party was sincere in this treaty ; for the conspirators expected aid from England, and the regent from France.   In the mean time, many protestants were obliged to take refuge in the castle, among whom was a preacher, named John Rough, who was made chaplain of the garrison.

Knox was residing at Langniddry, when

* Robertson's Hist. of Scotland, Book II.

the cardinal was put to death, instructing his pupils not only in the several branches of learning, but in the principles of the reformed religion. He used also publicly to catechise them, and to read and explain the Scriptures, in a chapel at Langniddry, which, though in ruins, is to this day called "John Knox's kirk." The new archbishop of St. Andrew's, irritated at the doctrines which Knox disseminated, soon raised a persecution against him, which obliged him to leave Langniddry, and retire to some place of safety. Wearied with the continual dangers which beset him, he resolved to withdraw to Germany, where the reformation was gaining ground. The reluctance of his pupil's parents, however, induced him to alter his purpose, and repair along with their sons to the castle of St. Andrews, where he continued to conduct the education of his charge in the same manner as he had done at Langniddry.

The lectures which Knox read in the castle chapel were accessible to all who chose to be present. His abilities were soon discovered, and his auditors earnestly entreated him to become the colleague of Rough, and enter on the duties of a public teacher. This he refused, assigning as his reason, that " he would not run where God had not sent him ;" meaning, that he did not consider himself as having a proper call to the work. This is a striking instance of humility in this reformer, and shows how averse he was to intrude himself into the sacred office.

The design, however, of making Knox accept the office of a preacher, was not laid aside. A consultation was held among the chief persons in the castle, when it was resolved that Rough should give him a public call in the name of the whole assembly. Accordingly, on the day appointed, Rough preached a sermon on the election of ministers, in which he showed, that a man who was fitted to instruct his brethren could not innocently refuse the office of teacher when called thereto. At the conclusion of the sermon, the preacher, turning to Knox, addressed him in the following words :—" Brother, you shall not be offended, although I speak unto you that which I have in charge ; even from all those that are here present, which is this :—in the name of God, and of his Son Jesus Christ, and in the name of those who call you by my mouth, I charge you

that you refuse not this holy vocation ;
but as you tender the glory of God, the increase of Christ's kingdom, the edification
of your brethren, and the comfort of me,
whom you understand well enough to be
oppressed by the multitude of labours, that
you take upon you the public office and
charge of preaching, even as you look to
avoid God's heavy displeasure, and desire
that he shall multiply his graces upon you."
Then addressing himself to the people, he
said, " Was not this your charge to me ?
and do ye not approve this vocation ?"
To which they replied—" It is, and we
approve it." Astonished at this unexpected charge, Knox burst into tears, and
withdrew to his chamber ; his countenance
and behaviour from that day to the day
that he was compelled to present himself
to the public place of preaching, sufficient-
ly declared the grief and trouble of his
heart ; a sadness seemed to pervade his
mind, and he remained alone for days together, deeply meditating on the importance and solemnity of the office which he
was about to assume.

Knox had now an opportunity of publicly defending the doctrines of the reformation, and of assisting Rough, who had

been violently, but weakly, attacked by
John Annan, dean of St. Andrew's. He
had assisted Rough with his pen, and,
laying the axe to the root of his adver-
sary's doctrine, had exposed the error of
Annan in a scriptural and masterly manner. At a public disputation, Knox boldly said to him, "As for your Roman
Church, as it is now corrupted, and the
authority thereof, wherein stands the hope
of your victory, I no more doubt but that
it is the synagogue of satan, and the head
thereof, called the pope, to be that man
of sin, of whom the Apostle speaketh, than
I doubt that Jesus Christ suffered by the
procurement of the visible church of Jeru-
salem. Yea, I offer myself, by word or
writing, to prove the Roman Church this
day farther degenerate from the purity
which was in the days of the apostles, than
was the church of the Jews from the ordi-
nances given by Moses, when they consented to the innocent death of Jesus
Christ." This bold averment had such an
effect upon the minds of the people who
were present, that they exclaimed, "We
cannot all read your writings, but we can
all hear your preaching : therefore we require you, in the name of God, that you

let us hear the proof of that which you have affirmed ; for if it be true, we have been miserably deceived."

Accordingly, on the following Sabbath, he ascended the pulpit, and preached his first sermon from Dan. vii. 24, 25, and fully redeemed his pledge ; proving from Scripture the anti-christian state of the church of Rome, and that " the life, doctrine, laws, and subjects" of its head were directly opposed to the true spirit of Christianity. Some who were present said, " he not only hewed the branches of papistry, but struck at the root also, to destroy the whole." Others said, " George Wishart never spoke so plainly, and yet he was burnt ; even so will he be." At the conclusion, Knox declared, that whoever conceived him to have given a wrong interpretation of Scripture, on coming to him he would give complete satisfaction. This sermon confirmed the faith of the friends of the reformation, and excited a great ferment among the adherents of popery.

The archbishop of St. Andrew's immediately wrote to the sub-prior Winram, who was a friend to the protestant doctrines, expressing his astonishment that he should allow such *heresies ;* and the sub-prior was, in consequence, obliged to call a convention of the popish clergy, before which Knox and Rough were summoned to appear. Among the charges produced against them were the following :—that they had said " No mortal man can be the head of the church—that the pope is an anti-christ, and so is no member of Christ's mystical body—that man may neither make nor devise a religion that is acceptable to God ; but man is bound to observe and keep the religion that from God is received, without changing thereof—that the mass is abominable idolatry, blasphemous to the death of Christ, and a profanation of the Lord's supper—that there is no purgatory in which the souls of men can be purged after this life—and, that praying *for* the dead is vain, while to pray *to* the dead is idolatry." After these and other charges had been brought against the two reformers, the sub-prior entered into an argument against Knox on some of the popish tenets ; which, after maintaining for some time, was taken up by a friar, who was soon obliged to abandon the dispute. The reformers were at last dismissed, with an admonition to beware what sort of doctrine they henceforth taught in public.

The catholic clergy, finding how much their cause was injured by these public examinations, issued orders for the learned men of the abbey and university to preach in the parish church on points that were not controverted, every Sabbath, by rotation. Perceiving this artifice, Knox, though deprived of the church on the Sundays, preached on the week-days. "He rejoiced," he said, "that Christ was preached, and that nothing was said against the doctrines of the reformation ; but," he added, "if in my absence they shall speak any thing which in my presence they do not, I protest that ye suspend your judgment till it please God that ye hear me again." In this way he continued his labours, and with such success, that very soon all the people in the castle, and many in the town, openly professed the reformed religion.

CHAPTER III.

The castle of St. Andrew's, besieged by a French fleet taken, and Knox, with the rest, made a prisoner and kept in confinement on board the galleys nineteen months, during which time he suffers many persecutions—Anecdote of his fearlessness and hatred to all manner of idolatry—Is liberated, and goes to England, where he preaches the gospel with great zeal—Becomes acquainted with the lady he afterwards marries.— Is made chaplain to the young prince, Edward VI.—Instance of Knox's zeal and disinterestedness—The accession of the 'Bloody Mary' to the throne of England obliges Knox to leave London ; but he continues to preach the gospel faithfully in different parts of the kingdom—Is obliged to fly to the continent—Receives a call to the church at Frankfort, to preach to those who, like himself, were compelled to take refuge in that city from the persecutions raging in their own country—Knox is falsely accused of treason—Turns his thoughts again to his native country.

KNOX continued in the faithful discharge of his ministerial duties till July, 1547. About the end of June, the castle was besieged by a French fleet, and was at last forced to surrender. Knox was put on board the fleet with the rest, and carried to France, where some were thrown into prison, while he, with several others, was confined on board the galleys for the space of nineteen months.

During this period, Knox suffered many hardships and insults on account of his religion. Every means was used to induce him and the other prisoners to countenance the errors of popery ; but even threatenings could not move them to the slightest concession. Soon after their arrival at Nantz, a circumstance occurred which is noticed by Knox himself in his "History of the Reformation," and it is believed that he is the individual himself, to whom he alludes. "A painted lady," says he, meaning a picture of the Virgin Mary, "was brought in to be kissed, and amongst others, was presented to one of the Scotsmen then chained. He gently said, 'Trouble me not ; such a jewel is accursed, and therefore I will not touch it.' The officers said, 'Thou shalt handle it ;' and they violently thrust it in his face, and put it betwixt his hands ; who seeing the extremity, took the idol and cast it into the river."

In the month of February, 1549, Knox was liberated from his prison, and immediately went to England. The duke of Somerset, at that time protector, and archbishop Cranmer, were friends of the reformation, and took him by the hand. By an order of council he was sent to preach at Berwick, where he continued, during the years 1549 and 1550, to discharge the duties of his office with much success, and was the instrument of convincing multitudes of the absurdities of popery, and leading them to embrace the simple truths contained in the Holy Scriptures. There were many catholics, however, in that part of the kingdom, who exerted every nerve to prevent the progress of what they called, " the new religion." Accordingly, on the 4th of April, 1550, he was summoned to appear before Tonstal, bishop of Durham, and a numerous assembly, where he defended his opinions with a strength of reasoning which so silenced his adversaries, that he was allowed to continue his ministry without further interruption.

It was at Berwick that he became acquainted with a young lady of the name of Marjory Bowes, to whom he was afterwards united in marriage. In 1551 he was appointed one of the chaplains to Edward VI., a pious and excellent young prince, with a pension of forty pounds (about 177 dollars) per annum. His zeal for the reformed religion, however, and the bold attacks which he had formerly made on the Romish superstitions, continued without the least abatement. In a sermon preached at Newcastle, in 1552, he affirmed that all who were despisers in heart of the gospel of Christ, as then preached in that kingdom, were the enemies of God, and traitors to the government, regardless who reigned, so they obtained the re-establishment of idolatry. The papists made a great handle of these words, and Knox was summoned to appear before the council at London; but, contrary to the wishes of his enemies, he was honourably acquitted.

The council, pleased with his services, presented him the living of All-hallows in London, which was then vacant; but the offer was decidedly refused by Knox, who on this occasion exhibited a noble instance of disinterestedness. Superior to every thing like ambition, he cheerfully sacrificed the highest worldly advantages. This became more evident at a future period, when he was offered a bishopric by king Edward, which he would not accept. His conduct, indeed, from first to last, bears testimony to the purity of his motives, and shows that all his anxiety was to rescue his country from the yoke of oppression.

In July, 1553, the bloody Mary ascended

the throne of England, and soon began a
persecution against the protestants, equal
in barbarity to the deeds of the greatest
tyrant that ever swayed a sceptre.   Knox
appears to have left London on her accession, and in various parts of the kingdom
preached the glad tidings of salvation to
multitudes of people.   The importance
of the work in which he was engaged,
and his earnest desire faithfully to discharge its duties, will appear from the following account of the manner in which
he reproached himself for consulting his
own comfort more than the people's spiritual welfare : " In preaching of Christ's
gospel, albeit mine eye, as God knoweth,
was not much on worldly promotion ; yet
the love of friends, and carnal affection
of some men with whom I was most familiar, led me to reside longer in one
place than another, having more respect
to the pleasure of a few, than the wants
of many.   That day I thought I had not
sinned, if I had not been idle : but this
day, I know it was my duty to have had
consideration how long I remained in one
place, and how many hungry souls were
in other places, to whom, alas ! none took

pains to break and distribute the bread of life.''

Knox's salary was now stopped ; but he continued, though at great risk, to labour till January,1554, when the persecution having become general, by the advice of his friends he left England, and crossed over into France. At Dieppe he wrote letters to his friends behind, exhorting them to continue steadfast in the truth, and from thence he proceeded to Geneva, at that time the asylum for numerous protestant exiles. Here he employed himself for some time in private study, meditation, and prayer ; but the congregation of English refugees at Frankfort, who had fled thither from the persecutions of Mary, having given him a call to become their pastor, he, after some hesitation, accepted it, and commenced his ministry in November, with the unanimous approbation of the people.

The church at Frankfort had been allowed to be formed at first, on the express condition that they should conform to the worship used by the French protestants, and while these orders were obeyed, that church enjoyed tranquillity. The happiness, however, which Knox had here,

when he commenced his labours, was very
soon interrupted.   Dr. Cox, preceptor to
king Edward VI. arrived at Frankfort,
with some others in March, 1555, and dif-
fering with Knox on some points deemed
important, formed an adverse party, and
accused him to the state of *high-treason*
against the emperor, Charles V., and his
son Philip.   The *treason* was, his having
preached, while in England, against the
proposed marriage between Philip and the
English queen ; and in the same sermon,
asserting that the emperor, who was a
bigoted catholic, " was no less an enemy
to Christ than Nero was." When it is
remembered that these words, strained to
the utmost by his accusers, were spoken
in a country not under the dominion of
the emperor, the absurdity of such a charge
against Knox at that time must be apparent ; and the accusation of Cox and his
faction seems to be a most treacherous
and unchristian act.

The magistrates, sensible of the malice
of Knox's accusers, and yet afraid of being
suspected of disaffection to the emperor, if
it were known that they suffered a person
to continue in a church under their authority, who had been charged with the

crime of treason, privately advised him to leave Frankfort; and accordingly, after delivering a farewell sermon in his own lodgings, to a number of his congregation, he departed on the 26th of March, and returned to Geneva, where he was received with kindness. From the time he had left Scotland, however, his thoughts had been constantly turned to the state of religion at home; and he resolved therefore now to visit his native country, and render all his aid to those who were there struggling against the supporters of ignorance and error, who laboured hard to crush the rising reformation.

CHAPTER IV.

Mary of Guise, the queen dowager, succeeds the earl of
Arran in the regency—Progress of the reformation—
Knox arrives in Edinburgh—His successful labours—
Requests the queen to hear him preach the reformed
doctrines—Her reply—Accepts a call from Geneva—
After his departure, is summoned before the popish clergy—Condemned and burnt in effigy at Edinburgh—
Is recalled to Scotland, but meets with difficulties and
impediments, and determines to remain in Geneva—In
1586, he assists in making a new translation of the
Bible—Writes a book against the practice of raising
females to the government of kingdoms—His motives
for so doing.

In the meantime, the reformation had
been making, by slow yet sure steps, considerable progress in Scotland ; and by a
singular disposition of Providence, the
very persons who were its enemies, were
made instruments for advancing the cause.
Mary of Guise, the queen dowager, desirous of dispossessing the earl of Arran
of the regency, and of succeeding him in
that high dignity, courted the protestants
with the greatest assiduity. She promis-
ed them every protection and indulgence
in their worship, and so far prevailed, as
to induce them to favour her pretensions.
At length, on the 10th of April, she succeeded in obtaining the consent of the earl
of Arran to resign the regency, and gained
the height of her ambition, by being placed

at the head of the nation. From the protection, which, during these intrigues, she afforded the protestants, the reformation gained additional strength, and began to spread in all quarters of the kingdom. The cruel persecutions too of the protestants by the English queen, compelled many reformers to take refuge in Scotland, where, by their zeal against popery, they greatly promoted the progress of pure religion.

Knox left Geneva, in August, 1555, and in a short time arrived at Edinburgh. On his arrival in Scotland, he found that the professors of the reformed religion had conformed in several points to the popish worship. The reasonings of Knox, however, soon led them to reject these as idolatrous and absurd; and thus at the very first, he effected a separation from the popish church, then established in his native country.

Soon after, he accompanied Mr. Erskine of Dun, to his estate in Angus-shire; where, during his stay of about a month, he preached the gospel to great numbers, both among the poor and the rich. On his return to the north, he resided at Calder-houp with sir James Sandilands, a man of great prudence, and attached to the protestant cause. Here he was visited by the master of Erskine, afterwards the earl of Mar ; lord Lorn, afterwards the earl of Argyle ; and lord James Stewart, afterwards the earl of Murray, and first regent, during the minority of James VI., who were all pleased with his doctrine, and zealously entered into his plans for a general reformation.

In the beginning of 1556 he was invited to Ayrshire, where he preached in many places with great success. In several, he administered the sacrament of the Lord's supper, after the manner of the reformed churches. Shortly afterwards, he paid a second visit to the laird of Dun, where he preached more openly than formerly. In short, multitudes, wherever he went, renounced the Romish worship, and professed the protestant faith.

The popish clergy, alarmed at the success of the reformer, after consulting together on the best mode of putting a stop to the protestant religion, summoned him to appear before them at Edinburgh, on the 15th of May. Not in the least intimidated, Knox obeyed, and went to Edinburgh, accompanied by the laird of Dun, and several other gentlemen who were determined to defend him against the malice of his enemies. The clergy, however, not expecting that he would have appeared, and afraid of the consequences if they should adopt any violent measures against him, under pretence of some error in the summons, deserted, or at least delayed the prosecution for the present. In consequence of this, the very day that he should have appeared before them as a criminal, he preached to a larger audience than had ever attended him in the metropolis on any former occasion.

At the request of the earl of Glencairn, the earl Marischal was prevailed on to hear the reformer preach, and was so well pleased with his discourse, that he insisted on Knox's writing a letter to the queen-regent, requesting her to hear the doctrines of the reformers. Knox was induced to comply ; but no sooner had she perused his letter, than turning to the archbishop of Glasgow who was with her when she received it, and putting it into his hand, she said, " Please you, my lord, to read a pasquil."*

About this time Knox received letters from the English protestants at Geneva,

* The word "pasquil" signifies a personal satire.

who had withdrawn from Frankfort when
he quitted that place, earnestly entreating
him to visit them and become one of their
pastors.   After seriously considering this
invitation, he determined to comply with
it, and taking leave of his friends in Scotland, he set out in July, 1556, for Geneva,
with his wife and mother-in-law, Mrs.
Borres.   No sooner did the bishops learn
that he had left the kingdom, than, in the
most shameful and cowardly manner, they
summoned him before them ; and on his
failing to appear, which they well knew
was wholly unavoidable, they sentenced
him to death, and caused his effigy to be
burnt at the cross of Edinburgh.   When
Knox heard of these unjust and weak
proceedings, he immediately wrote a severe appeal, in which he gives a distinct
account of the doctrines which he preached ; complains of the unfair treatment he
received from the popish clergy ; and requests the people of Scotland not to condemn him or the other reformers till the
points of controversy could be fairly de-
cided.

Knox continued at Geneva during two
years, in the course of which he had two
sons.   Enjoying the affection of his con-

gregation, this appears to have been the most tranquil period of his life ; and what still farther added to his happiness, he learned that the zeal and perseverance of the protestants in his native country remained unabated.

In April, 1567, he received a letter from Scotland, signed by the earl of Glencairn, lords Erskine, Lorn, and James Stewart, informing him, " that the faithful remained steadfast in the belief wherein he left them," and requesting him to return to his native country, where he would find them " not only glad to hear his doctrine, but also ready to jeopard their lives and goods for the setting forward of the glory of God." This letter he laid before the congregation ; and his friends told him, upon consultation, that " he could not refuse that vocation, unless he would declare himself rebellious unto his God, and unmerciful to his country." He accordingly returned an answer promising to visit them as soon as possible. Having provided, therefore, for his congregation, he left Geneva in October, and came to Dieppe in his way to Scotland. While there, however, he received other letters, informing him that some of the protestants were averse to his coming to that kingdom, and advising him to remain at Dieppe till he received more favourable information.

"Confounded," as he says himself, "and pierced with sorrow" at this unexpected intelligence, he immediately wrote to the lords who had given him the invitation, strongly expostulating with them on their inconstancy. He remained some time after this in France, and wrote several letters to Scotland, but receiving no intelligence, he returned to Geneva towards the close of the year 1557.

In 1558 he assisted in making a new translation of the Bible into English, which received the name of the Geneva Bible. In the same year he published a book, in which he vehemently condemns the practice of raising females to the government of kingdoms. It is supposed that the cruel and bloody government of Mary, queen of England, and the duplicity of the queen-regent of Scotland were the chief reasons which impelled him to this publication. John Fox, the martyrologist, however, in a letter to Knox, expostulated with him on the impropriety of publishing his "Blast." In his answer Knox apologized for whatever harsh or vehement expressions he

might have used in the heat of his zeal ;
but still affirmed that he was persuaded of
the chief positions which that treatise contained.

CHAPTER V.

A solemn covenant entered into to promote the Reformation—Its advancement—The queen-regent openly favourable, but secretly hostile to the cause—Her motives
—She throws off the mask—Persecutions—Inhuman
murder of the venerable Walter Mill—His prophetic
words at the stake—Wicked and unprincipled conduct
of the queen-regent—She summons all the protestant
pastors—The people resolve to defend their pastors—
Knox arrives at this critical moment—His bold eloquence,
and its effects—The mob, exasperated, commit outrages
which are severely censured by Knox—Civil war—The
treachery of the queen—Knox urged not to preach at St.
Andrew's on account of the danger from the queen's
army—His fearless reply and conduct—The queen's
purposes frustrated—Her perfidiousness—The protestant
army, exasperated, destroy all the monuments of Catholic
superstition they meet with on their march, but do not
persecute or put to death a single catholic.

THE various letters which Knox wrote
to Scotland greatly confirmed the protestants. They no longer countenanced the
worship of the church of Rome, and they
agreed that persons properly qualified
should be appointed to read the Scriptures
every Lord's-day ; that the sacrament
should be administered in a language which

could be understood; that the preaching and interpretation of Scripture should be in private, till they were permitted to meet in more public assemblies ; and that the regent should be solicited to grant them these indulgences. Besides these, they also entered into a solemn bond or covenant to promote the cause of the reformation; and, lastly, they wrote to Knox, beseeching him to return to Scotland.

In the mean while the reformation was still making progress, and its secret enemy, the queen-regent, from political causes, was under the necessity of wearing the mask a little longer, in order to accomplish her schemes. The young queen of Scots, Mary, had been sent to France at six years of age to be educated at the court, and given in marriage to the dauphin, and the regent was at this time extremely anxious to hasten the marriage. She accordingly affected to favour the protestants, and even granted them the free exercise of their religion, provided they did not hold any public assemblies at Leith or Edinburgh. Under these circumstances religion made a rapid progress ; but as soon as the artful regent attained her wishes, she began to throw off the mask.

The flames of persecution were rekindled by the popish clergy, who saw with alarm the progress of the reformation ; and they perpetrated an act which, though intended as a severe blow to the cause, ultimately proved their own ruin. This was the murder of Walter Mill, an aged priest, who had renounced the errors of popery in which he was educated. The archbishop of St. Andrew's caused him to be thrown into prison ; but when he was brought to trial, his venerable appearance excited the sympathy of all who saw him, except his inhuman persecutors. He meekly, but fearlessly defended himself, but in vain ; he was condemned to suffer death! The horror of the people was so great, that no temporal judge would pronounce the sentence of the ecclesiastical court, neither would the people supply ropes to bind him, or materials for his execution. A servant of the archbishop at length undertook to act the part of a secular judge, and the ropes of the archbishop's pavilion were all they could procure for binding this venerable martyr. On the 28th of August, 1558, the aged saint perished in the flames at St. Andrew's, after uttering these words : " I am now

eighty-two years old, and cannot live long
by the course of nature ; but a hundred
shall rise out of my ashes who shall scatter
you, ye persecutors of God's people.   I
trust in God I shall be the last who shall
suffer death for this cause in this land."

This shocking murder gave the death-
blow to popery in Scotland.   Nothing
could equal the horror of the protestants
at such a barbarous and illegal proceeding ;
and as they had no suspicion that the
queen-regent was accessory to the crime,
they applied to her for redress.   But she
was engaged, at this very time, in forming
secret plans with the archbishop for their
total ruin.

All the entreaties which the protestants
now made to be permitted to enjoy their
own worship were rejected with scorn ;
and soon afterwards the queen issued a
proclamation commanding all persons to
observe the approaching festival of Easter,
according to the Romish church.   This
order not being attended to by the protestants, she summoned their preachers
to answer for their conduct.   The earl
of Glencairn and sir Hugh Campbell of
London appeared on behalf of the protestants to expostulate with her on this

act of severity ; but she received them haughtily, and had the effrontery even to tell them, " that in despite of them and their ministers both, they should be banished from Scotland, although they preached as true as ever did the apostle Paul !" On their reminding her of her former engagements to grant them protection, she had the audacity to make the following reply : " The promises of princes ought neither to be remembered nor exacted, unless it suits their own convenience !"

The anger of the queen when she uttered this monstrous sentiment was nothing in comparison to the rage which she manifested when she heard that the inhabitants of Perth had renounced popery, and embraced the reformed religion. She immediately issued a mandate summoning all the protestant preachers to appear before a court of justice at Stirling Alarmed, but not intimidated, the protestants were resolved to defend their pastors to the utmost of their abilities ; and they accordingly assembled at Perth in great numbers. Such a multitude, though unarmed, alarmed the queen, and she employed Erskine of Dun, who was attached to the reformation, to promise in her name, that she would put a stop to the intended trial, provided they did not approach nearer Stirling. On this assurance the people quietly returned home ; but no sooner were they dispersed, than she broke her promise, and on the day appointed, all the preachers were condemned as outlaws for not appearing at the trial. The congregation, alarmed for their safety, as well as shocked at the conduct of the queen, again collected at Perth, and began to use means for averting the impending danger.

On the 2d of May, 1559, a few days only before the appointed trial at Stirling, Knox arrived at Edinburgh. He came, therefore, as he says himself, "even in the brunt of the battle." The popish council, which was assembled in the gray friars' monastery, having received notice of his arrival, were so disconcerted that they hastily closed their session, and retired with precipitation. Having lodged two nights at Edinburgh, Knox went first to Dundee and then to Perth, determined to assist his brethren, or share the dangers to which they were exposed. While he remained at Perth, on the arrival of the news that the queen had broken her promise, he immediately mounted the pulpit, and preached with boldness against the mass and the worship of images. His eloquence inflamed as well as convinced his hearers, and produced effects which though unintended by the minister, might have been naturally expected. When the sermon was over, and the greater part of the audience had retired, a Roman catholic priest, probably wishing to show his detestation of the doctrine which he had just heard, began to decorate the altar, for the purpose of celebrating mass. A boy who stood by boldly said, "This is too bad, that, when God by his word, hath plainly condemned idolatry, we should stand and see it used in spite." Offended at this remark, the priest struck the boy, who, in revenge, threw a stone at the priest, which broke one of the images. The people who were present, taking the boy's part, overturned the altar, demolished the images, defaced the pictures, and trampled their broken fragments in the dust. A mob collected, and being highly exasperated, they proceeded to the monasteries, which in a few hours they almost levelled with the dust.

Knox severely censured this violence, which was indeed solely to be attributed to the rage of the people at the perfidious conduct of the queen. She, however, considered it as a contempt of her authority as well as her religion, and was determined to take vengeance on the whole reformed body. She collected troops as quickly as possible, among whom were some French soldiers. The protestants, joined by a reinforcement under the earl of Glencairn, were soon in a condition to face the queen, who, instead of risking a battle, proposed terms, which were immediately accepted.

Though the protestants admitted her into Perth, and dispersed themselves; yet placing no reliance on the queen's word, before they dispersed they entered into a new bond to defend the common cause if she should violate the treaty. The queen, as was anticipated, no sooner obtained possession of the town, than she broke every condition of the treaty to which she had so solemnly agreed.

The earl of Argyle, and the prior of St. Andrew's, enraged at the perfidy of the queen, abandoned her, and joined the lords of the congregation, who had retired to St. Andrew's. Knox, being invited by

them to repair to that city, proceeded
thither without delay, preaching in Crail
and Anstruther by the way. Having
arrived at St. Andrew's, he signified his
intention of preaching the following day
in the cathedral, which being understood
by the archbishop, he assembled his troops,
and informed the heads of the congregation, that if " Knox offered to preach there,
he should have a warm military reception." Afraid of the consequences, the
lords advised Knox to defer preaching that
day, especially as the queen's army was
lying at a short distance. The bold answer of the reformer, which was some-
thing like that of Luther when dissuaded
from attending the diet at Worms, at once
silenced the remonstrances of his friends:
" God is my witness," said he, " that I
never preached Christ Jesus in contempt
of any man ; but to delay preaching to-
morrow *I cannot ;* for in this town and
church began God first to call me to the
dignity of a preacher, from the which I
was reft by the tyranny of France, and
procurement of the catholic bishops, as
ye know. Therefore, seeing that God,
above the expectation of many, hath
brought my body to the same place

where first I was called to the office of a preacher, and from which most unjustly I was removed, I beseech your honours not to stop me. And as for the fear of danger that may come, let no man be solicitous, for my life is in the custody of Him whose glory I seek ; and, therefore, I cannot so fear their boast nor tyranny that I will cease from doing my duty, when of his mercy he offereth me occasion. I desire the hand and weapon of no man to defend me ; I desire only to be heard, which if it be denied here unto me at this time, I must seek further where I may have it." He accordingly preached that and the three following days without interruption, and with so much success that the magistrates and inhabitants agreed to embrace the reformed religion, and to remove every vestige of idolatry.

Though the archbishop did not attempt to hinder Knox from preaching, he repaired to Falkland, where the queen's army was still lying. Having consulted together, the queen, imagining that she could easily crush the few protestants assembled at St. Andrew's, instantly put her troops in motion. The lords of the congregation, however, being informed of her

approach, apprized their brethren throughout the country. They then set out to
meet the queen with only one hundred
horse ; but as they advanced, crowds joined them ; and by the time they arrived at
Cupar-moor, which was only a few miles
distant, their force was much superior to
that of the queen-regent.

Frustrated in her intentions, she was
obliged again to have recourse to a nego-
tiation, in which she pretended to be very
desirous to settle all the differences existing between the parties. But this, like
all her other treaties, was soon violated ;
and the lords of the congregation, being
incensed, assembled their followers, compelled the garrison of Perth to surrender ;
and. afterwards seized upon the town of
Stirling, whose inhabitants gladly opened
their gates. They advanced rapidly towards Edinburgh, and, on the 29th of
June, took possession of that capital, which
the queen-regent hastily abandoned.

The queen retired to Dunbar ; and
wherever the protestant army came, the
monuments of catholic superstition were
destroyed. The churches were stripped
of their ornaments, and the monasteries
laid in ruins by the infuriated multitude,

in their zeal against popery. Yet in the
midst of this rage against superstition, it
should be remembered what is stated by
the celebrated historian, Dr. Robertson,—
" that few of the Roman catholics were
exposed to any personal insult, and not a
single man suffered death."*

CHAPTER VI.

The lords of the congregation appoint John Knox their
minister—Edinburgh taken by the queen's troops—Knox
travels over the kingdom preaching—Edinburgh retaken
and the regent deposed—Disasters to the protestant
cause—Knox revives his countrymen, and predicts their
final triumph—The protestants appeal to queen Elizabeth, who sends succours from England—Death of the
great enemy of the reformation, the queen-regent—Settlement of affairs—Parliament abolish the rites of the
Romish Church, and a " Confession of Faith," in the
drawing up of which Knox has a principal share,
solemnly ratified.

EDINBURGH was now chosen by the lords
of the congregation as their residence,
and John Knox was appointed their minister. In the mean time the heavy expenses
of the protestant army had thinned their
number, and compelled the greater part to
return to their habitations. The queen,
taking advantage of this circumstance,
took the opportunity of advancing sud-

* Hist. of Scotland.

denly upon Edinburgh, and thus brought
the inhabitants to terms which were more
favourable than might have been expected.

Knox wished to continue his preaching
at Edinburgh after the city was in the
hands of the regent; but the lords, appre-
hensive of danger, would not consent.
Another individual, John Willock, was
left in his place ; and Knox, leaving the
place with the lords, travelled over the
greater part of the kingdom, preaching the
gospel with such earnestness, that many
were led to reject the absurdities of the
Romish superstition.

A reinforcement of troops from France
gave new confidence to the queen, and
Knox did not escape her fury ; for, in the
height of her wrath, she offered a reward
to any individual who would apprehend
the reformer, or put him to death. The
injustice and wickedness of the regent had
grown to such a pitch, that the protestants
again marched upon, and took possession
of Edinburgh ; and assembling a convention of all the peers, barons, and repre-
sentatives who favoured the reformation,
after much deliberation on the measures
which it was necessary for them to take
under existing circumstances, they unani-

mously resolved to deprive the regent of
the office which she so unworthily exer-
cised. At this convention, Knox was
called upon to give his opinion as to the
lawfulness of so important a measure,
which he did fully.

The affairs of the protestants, however,
soon after took an unfavourable turn ; and
after several reverses and disasters, they
were at length compelled to leave Edinburgh, and retire in great confusion to
Stirling ; but during their calamities,
Knox spared no exertions to revive the
languid spirit of his countrymen. On
the very day after their arrival at Stirling, he preached a sermon which kin-
dled anew their zeal, and opened to their
minds prospects which roused them from
despondency. He had been preaching
on the 80th Psalm while in Edinburgh,
and he now finished his discourse on
verses 4—8, when he predicted the final
triumph of the cause in which they were
engaged :—" Our faces," said he, " are
this day confounded ; our enemies triumph ; our hearts have quaked for fear ;
and still they remain oppressed with sorrow and shame. But what shall we think
to be the true cause of God's having re-

jected us ? If I should say our sins and
former ingratitude, I should say the truth ;
but as yet I speak more generally than I
ought : for when the sins of men are re-
buked in general, it is seldom that man
brings it so home to himself, as to accuse
and condemn that in himself which is most
displeasing to God. Let us begin at our-
selves, who have been longest engaged in
this contest. When we were few in number compared to our enemies ; when we
had neither earl nor lord (a few excepted)
to comfort us, we called on God, and took
him for our protector, defence, and only
refuge. We did not boast of our numbers, our strength, or our wisdom ; but
only cried unto God to have respect to
the justice of our cause. But since our
number has increased, there has been nothing heard but,—this lord will bring us
so many hundred spears ;—this man has
eloquence sufficient to persuade multitudes
to join us ;—or, if this earl be on our side,
no man in such a district will trouble us.
And thus the best of us, who before experienced the powerful hand of God to be
our defence, have lately put trust in an
arm of flesh. But if we unfeignedly return to the Eternal, our God, I no more

doubt that this our grief, confusion, and fear, shall be turned into joy, honour, and boldness, than that God gave victory to the Israelites over the Benjamites, after they had been twice repulsed with ignominy. *Yea, whatever shall become of us and our mortal bodies, I doubt not but that this cause shall prevail in this realm. For as it is the eternal truth of the eternal God, so shall it finally prevail, though it be resisted for a season."*

The eyes of the protestants were now turned towards England, and they resolved to implore assistance from queen Elisabeth. Knox had formerly been employed to solicit aid from the English court, and through his means pecuniary assistance had been sent ; and although the money was intercepted, he encouraged the lords to renew the application. William Maitland, of Lethington, who was well qualified for the business, was despatched, and succeeded so well, that Elisabeth desired the lord to send commissioners to Berwick, where a treaty was finally settled in February, 1560.

The queen was now determined, if possible, to strike a decisive blow, and ruin the protestant army before they could obtain aid from England. Accordingly her troops marched to Stirling, destroying, plundering, and laying waste the country, in all directions with savage fury. As they were approaching St. Andrew's, which they intended to fortify, they beheld a fleet sailing up the Frith, transported at which, they began to fire guns of joy, imagining they were a fresh supply of troops from France ; but they were soon sadly disappointed to find that it was an English fleet come to the aid of the congregation ; and that a land army, also, had already begun its march into Scotland.

Events now assumed a very different aspect. The French troops of the regent were obliged rapidly to retreat ; they took refuge in Leith, where they were closely besieged ; and it was just at this crisis that it pleased Heaven to remove the queen-regent, who died in the castle of Edinburgh, where she had taken shelter. A treaty was immediately made ; the French troops left Scotland ; the nation was to have a free parliament till the arrival of their sovereign Mary ; and the protestants were not to be called to account for the part they had taken against

the late queen-regent. The protestant
nobility and a great part of the congregation met at St. Giles's church, to return thanks to God for the deliverance
they had experienced, and the rest He had
given to his afflicted and persecuted
church.

In August, 1560, the parliament met,
and a general petition was presented, praying that the doctrines and ceremonies of
the Romish church might be abolished ;
that the pope's authority might be renounced ; and the church revenues appro-
priated for the maintenance of the protestant ministers, and the support of the
poor. The parliament appointed the ministers to draw up a summary of the doctrines which they wished to be sanctioned ;
and in four days, they presented their
" Confession of Faith," which, being read,
was approved and solemnly ratified by
parliament, and appointed to be received
as the true confession of the protestant
faith over the kingdom. Knox had the
principal share in framing this confession,
which had been preparing a long time, a
circumstance which accounts for the short
time required for its completion. Thus,
after much labour and great struggles, the

contest between protestantism and popery was brought to a happy termination, by the reformed religion being established in Scotland.

CHAPTER VII.

Knox loses his wife—Apprehension of another invasion from France—Measures taken by Knox to secure the protestant religion—The death of Francis, husband of the young queen of Scots, breaks the bond which united the two countries—The arrival of Mary in Scotland—She hates the reformers, but is compelled to dissemble—Begins to disclose her real sentiments—Long and serious conversation between Knox and the young queen, who accuses him of exciting rebellion—He repels her charges with spirit—Knox forms an unfavourable opinion of the young queen Mary from this interview—He omits no occasion to proclaim the dangers to which the reformation was exposed—His plainness and severity properly explained and defended.

In December, 1560, Knox met with a severe affliction in the death of his wife, who appears to have been an amiable woman, and a partner in many of the troubles he endured. His grief was great ; but as he had often given comfort to others in distress, so he found in his own experience that consolation in affliction which can only be derived from the holy Scriptures. Mrs. Knox left behind her two young children.

Although the protestant religion had met with great success, there were still members in Scotland who adhered to the church of Rome. Mary, and her husband Francis too, had refused to acquiesce in the late treaty ; and a new army was raising in France for the purpose of assisting in the re-establishment of the catholic religion in Scotland. Foreseeing the danger, Knox endeavoured to procure a complete settlement of the reformed religion throughout the country. Accordingly, at a convention held in May, 1561, an act was issued, ordering every monument of idolatry within the kingdom to be demolished, and appointing proper persons to see this order put in immediate execution. Having thus received the authority of a public law, in a few weeks almost every popish edifice, however ancient or costly, was laid in ruins ; the people detesting the very houses in which idolatry and superstition had been practised.

But the fears of the reformers as to a new invasion of Scotland by France were disappointed ; for news arrived of the death of Francis, husband of Mary queen of Scots, which at once broke the chief bond which connected the two countries.

Mary now received an invitation to return to her native country, and assume the reins of government, which she accepted, and arrived at Leith on the 19th of August, 1561, after an absence of nearly thirteen years. She was welcomed by her subjects with every demonstration of joy ; and as they hoped that she would not only tolerate but patronize their religion, they were prepared to submit to her authority with cheerfulness and affection. But the queen of Scots had been educated in a court which was passionately attached to popery, and had early imbibed the strongest aversion to the reformed religion, which she determined, as speedily as possible, to drive from her kingdom. The number and power of the protestants obliged her at first to dissemble her intention, but she only waited a fit opportunity for crushing a religion which she counted to be heresy, and for re-establishing popery with all its superstitious appendages.

It was not long before Mary began to disclose her sentiments. On the very Sabbath after her arrival, she ordered mass to be celebrated in her chapel at Holyrood house. This excited the fears of the protestants, who, during the preparations for that service, collected in numbers about the palace, and expressed their disapprobation in murmurs and complaints. At length the crowd, seizing the wax candles which the servants were carrying through the court to the chapel, broke them in pieces, and would have proceeded to other outrages, if they had not been checked by the reformed leaders. Knox himself, in private conversation, endeavoured to appease the multitude; but on the following Sabbath, he showed his abhorrence of idolatry, by preaching a sermon against the mass, in the course of which he declared, that "a single mass was more fearful to him than if ten thousand armed men were landed in any part of the country, for the purpose of crushing their religion."

Knox, as may be supposed, was an object of great dislike to the queen; who not long after her arrival, sent for him to the palace, and entered into conversation with him, hoping to subdue or overcome the bold spirit of the reformer. She accused him of having excited rebellion among her subjects; of having written a book against her authority; and

of being the cause of sedition even in
England. To these charges Knox fearlessly replied, "If to teach the truth of
God in sincerity—if to rebuke idolatry,
and to exhort the people to worship God
according to his word, be to raise rebel
lion, I certainly am liable to the charge ;
for it has pleased God of his mercy, to
make me an instrument of showing to
my countrymen the falseness of popery,
the deceit, the pride, and the tyranny of
the Roman antichrist. But if the true
knowledge of God, and the appointed
mode of worshipping him, be powerful
motives to loyalty and submission, in what
am I blameable ? I am persuaded your
grace has had, and at present has, more
unfeigned obedience, from those who profess the truth in Christ, than ever your
father or your ancestors had." The other
charges he also repelled with equal spirit
and propriety.

She next accused him of teaching the
people a different religion from that of
their sovereign, and inquired, "How can
such a religion be true, seeing *God com-
mands subjects to obey their princes ?*"
To this Knox replied that, "as true religion does not depend upon the authority

of earthly princes, but on that of the
eternal Jehovah, subjects cannot be justly
required to accommodate their religion to
the taste of their rulers ; for the history
of the church, both before and after the
death of our Lord, clearly proves that
princes are far more ignorant of true religion than their subjects.   To prove
which, he instanced the cases of Daniel
and his three brethren, who, though subject to the kings of Babylon, would not
consent to change their religion ; and also
the Israelites in Egypt, who detested the
abominable worship of Pharaoh and the
Egyptians."—" Yes," rejoined the queen,
" but none of these men raised the sword
against their rulers."—" Yet, madam,"
replied Knox, " you cannot deny but that
they resisted ; for those that obey not
the commandments that are given, in some
sort resist."—" But yet," said she, " they
resisted not by the sword."—" God, madam," returned Knox, " had not given
them the power and the means."—" And
do you think," said the queen, " that
subjects who have the power may draw
the sword against their princes ?"—" If
princes," replied Knox, " exceed their
bounds, they may be resisted even by

power ; for there is no greater honour and obedience to be paid to princes, than God hath commanded to be given to father and mother. If children join together against a father stricken with a phrensy and seeking to slay his children, apprehend him, take the sword from him, bind his hands, and put him in prison till his phrensy overpass, do they any wrong ? or will God be offended with them for hindering their father from committing horrible murder ? Even so, madam, if princes will murder the children of God, their subjects, their zeal is but a mad phrensy. To take the sword from them, to bind them, and to cast them into prison, till they be brought to a sober mind, is not disobedience, but just obedience, because it agrees with the will of God."

The queen at length said, " Then I perceive my subjects are to obey you, and not me ; and that they are to do what they please, and not what I command : I must therefore be subject to them, and not they to me."—" God forbid," replied Knox, " that I should ever command any to obey me, or set subjects at liberty to do whatever they please ; my desire is, that both princes and subjects may obey God.

And do not think, madam, that you receive wrong, when you are required to be subject to God, and to obey Him who requires kings to be fathers and queens to be mothers to the church."—" But yours is not the church I will nourish," rejoined the queen, " I will defend the church of Rome, for I think it is the true church of God."—" Your will, madam," said the reformer, " is no reason, neither doth your thought make the Roman church to be the true and immaculate spouse of Christ, for it is altogether polluted both in doctrine and manners ; yea, madam, I offer myself further to prove, that the church of the Jews who crucified Christ was not so far degenerated from God, as the church of Rome is declined."—" My conscience is not so," replied the queen.—" Conscience, madam," said Knox, " requires knowledge, and I fear that right knowledge you have none."—" But," said she, " I have both heard and read."—" So, madam," returned Knox, " did the Jews who crucified Christ, read both the law and the prophets, and heard the same interpreted in their own way. Have you heard any teach but those who are allowed by the pope and cardinals ? You may be assured *they* will speak nothing against their own estate."—" You interpret the Scripture," said the queen, " one way, and they in another : whom shall I believe, and who shall be judge ?"—" You shall believe God," replied Knox, " who plainly speaks in his word ; and farther than the word teaches, you are neither to believe the one nor the other." After some further conversation the queen observed, that if some whom she had heard were present, they would easily confute him. To which Knox eagerly replied, " Would to God, madam, that the most learned papist in Europe were present, and that your grace would patiently hear the reasonings of both sides to the end ; for I am persuaded that you would perceive the vanity of the popish religion, and how contrary it is to the Holy Scriptures. But the ignorant papist cannot, and the learned and crafty will not reason, neither suffer the grounds of their religion to be strictly inquired into. For they know that they are never able to sustain an argument, except fire and sword and their own laws be judges." When taking leave of the queen, he said, " I pray God, madam, that you may be as blessed within the commonwealth of

Scotland (if such be the will of God) as
Deborah was in the commonwealth of
Israel."

The protestants had expected very favourable results from this interview ; but
Knox formed a different opinion of Mary,
and informed his friend in private that she
was too blindly attached to popery, to permit a hope that she would alter her sentiments, or change her conduct towards the
reformed religion.   " If there be not in
her," said he, " a proud mind, a crafty
wit, and an indurate heart against God and
his truth, my judgment faileth me."

Knox was very fearful that the insinuating manners of the queen would abate the
zeal of the protestant nobility, and therefore he omitted no occasion to proclaim
the dangers to which he conceived the reformation was exposed.   The plainness
of the reformer to the queen has very often
been censured, but if one reflects upon the
precarious state in which the protestant
religion then was, and on the bloody and
intolerant spirit of popery of which the
nation had had such melancholy proofs,
and which the queen and many of the nobility were still struggling to revive ; instead of condemning, we must rather ad-

mire and approve the firmness and intrepidity of the reformer, to which, under the blessing of almighty God, Scotland is indebted for the civil and religious liberties by her, at this very day, enjoyed.

CHAPTER VIII.

Wicked joy manifested by the queen when she hears that the protestants were persecuted and murdered in France —Knox preaches on the occasion, and gives offence—Is summoned before the queen, and defends himself against his calumniators—Solemn agreement entered into at Kyle and Galway to defend the reformation—Unwearied watchfulness of Knox over the church—Resistance to the encroachments of papacy—Anger of the queen at Knox for publicly preaching against her intended marriage with a papist—Their conversation—She wishes to punish Knox, but is afraid of the people—Violent measures of the people to prevent the queen's domestics from celebrating mass at the palace—Knox accused of high-treason—His trial—Violence of the queen against him—His defence—He is unanimously acquitted by the lords—Testimony of the bishop of Ross, a zealous papist, in favour of the reformer.

In the year 1562, the queen received tidings from her popish friends in France that they were gaining strength, and that they had begun to persecute and murder the protestants ; which so pleased her that she gave a ball, and exhibited the most unfeigned joy. This excited great indigna-

tion among the people, and Knox on the
following Sabbath preached a sermon, in
which he particularly inveighed against
the oppression, the ignorance, and the
vanity of princes, their fondness for pleasure, and their joy at the afflictions of
God's people. The reformer was summoned to appear before the queen, at the
palace, next day. To her accusation of
his speaking irreverently, and endeavour-
ing to expose her to the contempt of her
subjects, Knox replied that his words had
been misrepresented ; in proof of which
he entreated her to hear what he had
preached as far as he could recollect it.
He accordingly repeated it, and when
finished, he challenged those who were
present to accuse him of having said any
more. The queen was obliged to acknowledge she had received a false report. " I
know," she added, " that my uncles and
you are not of one religion, and therefore
I cannot blame you, although you have no
good opinion of them ; but if you hear
any thing concerning myself with which
you are offended, come yourself and tell
me, and I will listen to you." To which
the reformer answered : " That the house
of Guise was the enemy of God and of

Christ, and he was sure their designs would be overthrown. He was willing to do any thing for her contentment which was not contrary to his office, and if her majesty would attend his public discourses, or appoint a time for hearing the substance of the protestant faith, he would cheerfully wait on her ; but to come merely to her chamber door, and to have no liberty but to whisper his sentiments, and inform her what others said and thought of her conduct, was inconsistent with his duties as a Christian minister."

At Kyle and Galloway, where Knox preached this year, he showed so plainly the dangers to which the protestant religion was exposed, that the gentlemen of that district entered into a solemn agreement to maintain the reformed faith, and to defend its ministers and friends by every lawful means in their power. In the mean time intrigues of all kinds were on foot to destroy the reformation, and to rid the queen of the protestants who surrounded her ; but Knox kept a watchful eye over the church, and exerted all his powers to baffle the wicked schemes of its enemies.

The catholics now began to preach with

great freedom and zeal, and in 1563, the popish priests became so bold as openly to celebrate mass in different parts of the kingdom. The protestants in the west, knowing that any applications from them would be disregarded by the queen, proceeded to execute the former proclamations against idolatry, and had some of the priests taken up. The queen, highly enraged, but fearful of openly showing resentment, sent for Knox in May, hoping to soften him into compliance with her wishes to favour the popish clergy. Knox told her, that if she would execute the laws, the protestants, he was sure, would never disturb the public peace; but if she acted otherwise, he believed, there were some who would not let the papists offend without being punished. He told the queen that they had acted in the west according to express acts of parliament, and then concluded with these words :—" It will be useful for your majesty to consider what your subjects may reasonably expect of your majesty; and how the mutual contract between you should lead you to act. They are bound to obey you, but ' only in the Lord.' You are bound to observe the laws towards them. You require them to serve you; they require from you protection and defence against wicked doers. Now, madam, if you deny your duty to them, which particularly requires you to punish idolaters, can you expect complete obedience from them? I fear not."

The queen acted with a great deal of dissimulation, and indeed carried her deceit so far, that she caused several of the papists who had celebrated mass to be apprehended and put into prison. The fact was, that a meeting of the parliament was soon expected, and she was afraid the protestants would propose to ratify the treaty of Leith, which would establish by law the reformed religion.

On the 26th of May the parliament did meet, and so much influence had the queen acquired over the nobles, that in all the acts which were passed, they seemed to take very little interest in the prosperity of the reformation. Knox remonstrated with several of the members, particularly with the earl of Murray, but his expostulations proving vain, he renounced the friendship of the earl, and continued at variance with him for nearly two years. Previous to the rising of the parliament,

he preached a sermon in presence of many
of the members, in which he accused the
nobles of ingratitude, and of cowardly
deserting the cause of Christ; and at the
conclusion, adverting to the reported marriage of the queen with a papist, he exclaimed—" This I will say, my lords, that
whensoever the nobility of Scotland, who
profess the Lord Jesus, consent to have
an infidel for their king, you will do all
that is in your power to banish Christ
from this realm;—you will bring the
vengeance of God on the country, a
plague upon yourselves, and, most probably, will add little to the happiness of
your sovereign."

When it was told the queen that Knox
had preached against her marriage, he was
summoned to appear before her, when
she, bursting into tears, with great vehemence accused him of insulting her character and her government. Waiting till
she was somewhat composed, Knox calm-
ly replied, " that although they had been
at different times engaged in controversy,
he had never formerly seen her offended
at him. But when it should please God
to deliver her from that bondage of darkness and error in which she had been edu-

cated, she would not consider the liberty
of his tongue offensive. When out of the
pulpit, he believed he had given offence
to few ; but when in it he was not his own
master ; on the contrary, he was bound to
obey Him who commanded him to speak
plainly, and to flatter no person on the
face of the earth."—" But what have you
to do with *my marriage ?*" rejoined the
queen. Knox was proceeding to show the
extent of his office as a minister of the gospel, and the reasons which led him to in-
troduce this subject in the pulpit, when the
queen interrupted him by again exclaiming, " What have you to do with my marriage ?" and in a tone of indignation and
contempt, " What are you in this commonwealth ?"—" A subject born within
the same, madam," replied Knox, offended
at the scornful manner of the queen, " and
though I be neither earl, lord, nor baron
within it, yet has God made me (however
abject I be in your eyes) a profitable member within the same. Yes, madam, to me
it appertains no less to forewarn of such
things as may hurt it, if I foresee them,
than it doth to any of the nobility ; for
both my vocation and conscience demand
plainness of me ; and therefore, madam, to

yourself I say what I spoke in public. Whensoever the nobility of this realm shall consent that you be subject to an unfaithful husband, they do as much as in them lieth to renounce Christ, to banish his truth from them, to betray the freedom of this realm, and, perchance, shall in the end do small comfort to yourself." The queen again burst into tears, and continued sobbing and crying for some time ; during which, Knox remained silent, and with an unaltered countenance. At last he said, " Madam, before God, I declare I never delighted in the weeping of any of God's creatures ; yea, I can scarcely abide the tears of my own boys when I correct them, much less can I rejoice in your majesty's weeping. But seeing that I have offered you no just occasion to be offended, but have spoken the truth as my vocation requires, I must sustain (although unwillingly) your majesty's tears rather than hurt my conscience, or betray the commonwealth through my silence." The queen, more than ever enraged, dismissed him from her presence, to wait her pleasure in another room ; where he, desirous of using every occasion to do good to others, employed the interval in preaching with great faithfulness to the ladies of the court. In the mean time, the queen consulted her lords and courtiers on the propriety of punishing him ; but they advised her not to do so, his power and influence rendering such a measure extremely dangerous. She was thus from necessity obliged to pass over the offence without farther censure, and the reformer was permitted to return to his home. So, to use Knox's own words, " that storm quieted in appearance, but never in the heart."

While the queen was residing in Stirling castle, her domestics at Holyrood house took it into their heads to celebrate mass more openly than when she had been present. Several protestants, being highly offended, went to the palace to see if the inhabitants joined in the Romish worship, and on seeing numbers entering the chapel, they themselves rushed in, and one individual boldly demanded, " how they dared in so open a manner, and in the absence of the queen, to break the laws of the land ?" In the mean time, the priest and mistress of the house, greatly alarmed, sent a messenger to an officer in the neighbourhood, desiring him to come instantly and save the queen's palace. He lost no

time in obeying the order, but when he
arrived at the palace, he found no appearance of riot or of danger. Two protestants were seized by order of the queen,
who was determined to punish them, and
they were to be subjected to a trial. The
danger of these two individuals alarmed
all the protestants, and they directed Knox
to issue letters to the chief persons pro-
fessing the true religion, requesting them
to assemble at Edinburgh on the day of
trial. A copy of this letter fell into the
queen's hands, and her council pronounc-
ing it treason, a prosecution was begun
against Knox ; and to render it more solemn and public, all the counsellors and
other noblemen were summoned to be
present on the day of trial, which was to
take place about the end of December.
Previous to this, however, various me-
thods were resorted to, for the purpose of
intimidating the reformer, and leading
him to acknowledge that he had committed an offence against the queen. But
all was insufficient to move the undaunted
spirit of Knox to confess a fault, when his
" conscience testified there was none."—
" I have given no occasion to the queen's
majesty," said he, " to be offended with

me ; for I have done nothing but my duty ; and therefore, whatever shall befall me, my hope is, that my God will give me patience to bear it."

When the day of trial arrived, great numbers flocked anxiously to the palace, to learn the result. As the reformer entered the room where the lords were assembled, the queen, looking at him while he approached the table, burst into laughter, exclaiming, "That man made me weep and never shed a tear himself, *but I will see if I can make him weep.*" He was then charged by the secretary as the author of the late tumult, and with assembling the queen's subjects without her authority, which was considered treason. The letter was then shown him, and he immediately acknowledged that it was his ; he even read it aloud at the desire of the queen, and afterwards returned it to the secretary. "Heard ye ever, my lords," said she, " a more despiteful and treasonable letter ?" The secretary then asked Knox if he was not sorry, and did not repent that such a letter ever came from his pen. " Before I repent," said Knox, " I must be taught my offence ; for your lordships must bear in mind, that there is a wide distinction between a lawful and an unlawful convocation. If I have been guilty in this, I have been often guilty since I last came to Scotland." To this the secretary replied, in a taunting manner, "Then was then, but then is not now. We have no need of such convocations as we formerly had."—"The time that has been," said the reformer, with animation, "is even now before my eyes ; for I see the poor flock in no less danger than it has been at any time before, except that the devil has got a mask upon his face. Before, he came in with his own face, seeking the destruction of all those who refused idolatry, and then I think you must confess the brethren assembled lawfully for defence of their lives. And now the devil comes disguised, under the mantle of justice, to do that which God would not suffer him to do by strength." The queen, indignant at his freedom, broke forth—"What is this ?" said she ; "who gave *him* authority to make convocation of my subjects ? *Is not that treason ?*"—"No, madam," said lord Ruthven, "for he makes convocation to hear prayer and sermon almost daily, and whatever your grace or others may think of it, we think it not treason."—"*Hold your peace,*" said she, "*and let him answer for himself.*" The reformer then resumed the subject, by declaring that the difference between a lawful and unlawful convocation was amply shown by lord Ruthven's observation, which, if the queen would deny, he would set himself to work to prove. "I will say nothing against your religion," said she, "nor against your convening to your sermons : but what authority have you to convene my subjects at your will, and without my commandment ?"—"At my will," replied Knox, "I never convened four persons in Scotland ; but at the order which the brethren have appointed, I have given divers notices, and great numbers have assembled. If your grace complain that it has been done without your commandment, I answer, so has all that God has blessed within this realm ; and therefore, madam, I must be convicted by a just law, of having acted contrary to the duties of a faithful messenger of God in writing this letter, before I be either sorry or repent for doing it ; for what I have done, I have done at the commandment of the general church of this realm."—"You shall not escape so," said the queen, and here she made great exertions to prove that Knox was guilty of treason for having accused her of *cruelty*, to establish which charge reference was made to certain acts of parliament. When the expression in Knox's letter, which was violently construed by the queen as an imputation of cruelty against her, was read, the whole assembly turned to the reformer in expectation of his reply. After a few preliminary remarks, in which he appealed to the queen to know if she was ignorant that the papists of that period were deadly enemies to all who professed the gospel, and desired the extermination of all who supported the reformed doctrines ; finding her majesty not able or not willing to make any reply, he continued. " I must proceed then," said he, " seeing all must grant it were a barbarous cruelty to destroy such a multitude as profess the gospel of Christ within this realm, they have had recourse to cunning and deceitful practices, to make the prince a party under colour of law ; so that what they could not do by force might be performed by fraud. For who believes that the cruelty of the papists will end with the murder of these two brethren now unjustly summoned and accused. And who does not know that by this proceeding they are only preparing a way for the destruction of the whole. Therefore, madam, cite your acts of parliament as you will, I have offended against none of them. I accuse not in my letter your grace, nor do I charge your nature with cruelty ; but I affirm that the papists who inflamed your grace without cause against these poor men are the sons of the devil, and, therefore, must obey their father, who has been a liar and a murderer from the beginning."—" You forget yourself," said one of the lords, " you are not now in the pulpit."—" I am in a place," replied Knox, " where I am demanded of conscience to speak the truth, and therefore the truth I will speak, let who will oppose it." He then addressed the queen, adding that evil counsellors had often corrupted those who appeared to be of gentle natures ; and that such were the papists to whom she had listened.

The queen then began to upbraid him with his former treatment. " You speak fair enough here before the lords," said she, " but the last time I spoke with you secretly, you caused me to weep many salt tears, and said to me you did not care for my weeping." Here Knox was obliged, in self-defence, to go over the whole of that scene which has been already detailed. After this the reformer was set at liberty to return home for that night.

As soon as he departed, the votes were taken whether he was guilty or not, and the lords unanimously agreed that he had committed no offence. The mortification of the queen was extreme when she found that her enemy was acquitted. To the bishop of Ross, who was himself a zealous papist, but who had voted in favour of Knox's innocence, she used the most upbraiding language ; but the bishop coolly replied, that it could neither be affection to the man, nor love to his profession, but the simple truth that appeared in his defence, that led him to vote for his acquittal. Thus did God once more defeat the designs of queen Mary against the great Scottish reformer.

CHAPTER IX.

The assembly solemnly approve of Knox's late conduct—
He marries a second time—Conference with Maitland—
Marriage of the queen with Darnley—Civil war—Bad
character of Darnley—Takes offence at Knox, who is
summoned before the council, and forbid to preach while
their majesties remained in Edinburgh—Machinations
of the papists—Murder of David Rizio, the queen's
favourite—The queen's hatred of her husband and
attachment to Bothwell—Horrible murder of Darnley,
in which Mary and Bothwell are believed to have taken
a part—The queen marries Bothwell—Civil war ensues
—The queen and Bothwell defeated—The latter obliged
to fly; while Mary surrenders herself prisoner to her
own subjects—The queen imprisoned in the castle of
Lochleven, and compelled to resign the crown to her
son James—The good earl of Murray appointed regent
during the minority of the young King—Subsequent
career, and dreadful fate of the wicked Bothwell.

On the following December, 1563, when
the assembly met, after the principal business of the meeting was transacted, Knox
called the attention of the members to his
late trial, and although some of the courtiers were unwilling to enter upon the
discussion, yet the assembly took up the
subject and solemnly acquitted him of all
the charges. They also declared that instructions had been given to the reformer
to notify the brethren when he was appre-
hensive of danger, and that he had acted
under their authority when he issued the

circular letters, on account of which he
had been brought to trial.

In March, 1564, Knox entered into the
married state a second time, after he continued a widower more than three years.
His second wife was Margaret Stewart,
daughter of lord Ochiltree, who was zealous in the cause of the reformed religion,
and much attached to Knox.   Not long
after this Knox was summoned to a conference (according to the custom of those
times) with Maitland the queen's secretary, and a very cunning disputant, where
he was accused of having spoken in the
pulpit disrespectfully of the queen, and
especially of using improper language in
his public prayers for her majesty ; but
he avoided the snares laid for him by his
great caution, and the conference broke
up without any serious consequences.

The queen's marriage in July, 1565,
with Darnley, who was a professed Roman
catholic, alarmed the protestants, and incensed the nobility who were attached to
the reformed doctrines.   Darnley, who
was the eldest son of the earl of Lennox,
was naturally of a most haughty and over-
bearing temper, and the present elevation
to which he was raised increased his pride

to a degree that rendered it almost intole-
rable. The queen's conduct, too, in pro-
claiming him king of Scotland, without
the consent of the estates, increased the
anger of the nobles, and led them to publish a declaration of their grievances, in
which they stated the insult which had
been done to parliament, as well as to religion, by this illegal measure. The earl
of Murray especially expressed his de
cided disapprobation of the marriage,
which excited the bitter resentment of
Darnley; and Murray having refused to
attend a convention at Perth, from just ap-
prehensions of danger, he was declared an
outlaw. Murray, and the other lords who
adhered to him, assembled at Stirling, and
after resolving to implore the protection
of Elizabeth, queen of England, they returned home. Queen Mary, however,
ordered her forces to march against them,
when they were compelled to take up
arms in self-defence, and, although they
used every exertion to bring about a reconciliation, they found the queen was ob-
stinately bent on their destruction. They
accordingly took shelter in England.

Darnley was a papist by profession, but
in reality possessed no religion. He could

celebrate mass with the queen, or attend the service of the reformers, just according to the circumstances in which he was placed. To soothe the protestants, and with the pretence of showing that he had no hostility to their religion, he went in great pomp to the church of St. Giles on the 19th of August. Knox preached from Isaiah xxvi. 13, 14, "O Lord, our God, other lords beside thee have had dominion over us," &c.; and in the course of the sermon he took occasion to speak of the government of wicked princes whom God sometimes raised up to scourge a people for their sins. Although there was nothing directly personal in what the preacher said, yet the king applied certain passages to himself, and returned to the palace in great indignation.

Knox was called before the council again, and for the offence he had given, they ordered him not to preach while the king and queen remained in the city. To this command he replied that "he had spoken nothing but according to his text; and if the church would order him either to speak or abstain, he would obey as far as the word of God would permit him." The queen, however, was greatly enraged

at an expression afterwards used by Knox
—whereupon he was absolutely forbid
preaching by the council. But their majesties having left Edinburgh before the
following Sabbath, the injunction laid upon
Knox to abstain from preaching lasted but
a very little while, and he proceeded in
the lofty duties to which he was summoned
from on high with indefatigable zeal.

At this period the protestant religion
was exposed to very great danger from the
evil designs of the queen, which justly
alarmed the reformers. The most powerful nobles who favoured the protestant
faith were driven into banishment, and the
queen sought to snatch a favourable occasion to establish the popish worship
throughout the kingdom. The king and
many of the nobility openly celebrated
mass; and Mary had subscribed her name
to a copy of the league which had been
sent from France for destroying all who
professed the reformed worship. The ex-
iled lords were summoned to appear before the parliament, which was to meet in
March; and the queen, for the purpose of
completely establishing her own religion,
had several altars prepared, which were

intended to be erected in the church of St. Giles, in order to celebrate the mass.

But all these pernicious designs were suddenly frustrated by the unexpected murder of an individual named Rizio, a worthless favourite of the queen. He was a foreigner of low birth, but of agreeable and insinuating manners, and having gained the favour of the queen, he treated every one with an unbecoming insolence, which greatly angered the nobility. Being at the same time an avowed enemy to the reformed religion, and a chief instigator of the queen against the banished lords, the resentment of some of the nobles carried them so far, that they resolved to destroy him ; and they were not long in putting into execution their wicked purposes. At the head of this conspiracy was Darnley himself, who had now lost the affections of Mary, which he ascribed chiefly to the influence which Rizio had gained over her. As soon as Rizio was put to death, the banished lords returned to Scotland. But the king, shortly after this, practising great deceit on the occasion, utterly denied all knowledge or participation in the matter, in consequence of which, the other conspirators, to avoid the vengeance of the queen, were compelled to seek refuge in England. These events, however, had the good effect of putting an end, at least for the present, to the queen's evil intentions against the protestant religion.

In 1566 Knox received permission from the general assembly to visit his two sons, who were then at the university of Cambridge ; and it was during his absence in England that the queen acted a part which proved the cause of all her subsequent misfortunes, and at last brought her to an untimely and dreadful end. Her affection for Darnley, which had greatly decreased soon after their marriage, was turned into deep and rankling hatred from the moment of the murder of her favourite Rizio. Although the birth of her only son James was the cause of great joy to the nation, it produced no reconciliation between her and the king. In the mean while the earl of Bothwell had now completely gained the affections of Mary ; and she not only loaded him with marks of her bounty, but raised him to the highest offices of honour and importance.

In this manner, after showing a most determined hatred and aversion to her husband, the queen all at once and in a very extraordinary way pretended to be reconciled to him. She visited him at Glasgow, and, by her artful persuasions, prevailed on him to accompany her to Edinburgh. A house was prepared for his reception at a place called the Kirk of Field, in a solitary spot, where the queen attended him with the utmost care. In the midst of all these suspicious proceedings, on the night of the 9th of February, he was barbarously murdered along with a servant, the house in which he lay being blown up with gunpowder. No person doubted that Bothwell was the chief contriver and executor of the murder : and the queen herself was suspected of being concerned in this detestable crime. Indeed, the behaviour of Mary from first to last towards her husband, and especially her marriage with Bothwell immediately afterwards, who was evidently the murderer, and who had lately been divorced from his wife, all confirm the testimony of the most respectable historians, who declare that the queen not only knew, but that she sanctioned the whole horrible transaction.

Knox was absent at the time the marriage between the queen and Bothwell was celebrated, and his colleague Craig, being commanded to publish the banns, informed the congregation that he had received such an order ; but that he not only declared the marriage to be unlawful, but took heaven and earth to witness that he detested it as "scandalous and infamous," and desired the nobles to use every endeavour to prevent it from taking place. For this he was twice called before the council, and charged with having exceeded the bounds of his commission. To which he replied, that the bounds of his commission were the word of God, natural reason, and good laws ; "by all which," said he, "I will make good that this marriage, if it proceed, will be hateful and scandalous to all that shall hear of it."

This marriage gave great dissatisfaction to the nation ; and excited the indignation of the nobles, especially when they learned that Bothwell was desirous of obtaining possession of the person of the young prince, whom they were afraid he would destroy, as he had already done his father. Accordingly, the nobles having entered into an association at Stirling for

defence of the prince, the queen and Bothwell took alarm, and hastily collected an
army to secure themselves against the storm
which began to blacken around them.
They first retired to the castle of Borth-
wick, but that place being invested by
part of the forces of the confederate lords,
Bothwell fled to Dunbar, and was fol-
lowed by the queen disguised in men's
clothes. Having assembled forces at
Dunbar, Bothwell and the queen marched
against the confederates, when, after an
ineffectual attempt at an accommodation,
Bothwell was obliged secretly to fly from
the field, while the queen surrendered
herself prisoner to her own subjects. This
dismal reverse, it is observed by an historian, happened exactly one month after
that marriage which had cost Bothwell so
many crimes to accomplish, and which
leaves so foul a stain on the memory of
Mary.

After some deliberation, the lords imprisoned the queen in the castle of Lochleven, where they obliged her to resign
the crown to her son, and to appoint the
good earl of Murray regent, till James
was of age to take the government of the
kingdom into his own hands. The young

prince was accordingly crowned shortly afterwards, and all public transactions of the nation were in future carried on in his name.

It may be instructive to the young reader to learn the subsequent career and ultimate fate of the wicked Bothwell. Finding it impossible to remain safely in Scotland, he fled to the Orkney Isles, and soon afterwards put to sea as a pirate ! Having attacked a vessel richly laden on the coast of Norway, the Norwegians sailed to its assistance, and succeeded in securing Bothwell and all his crew, whom they carried to Denmark. There he was cast into prison ; and after ten years confinement, during which he entirely lost his reason, he ended a miserable life, loaded with crime, and unpitied by a single human being !

CHAPTER X.

IT was about the period of the queen's
flight with Bothwell to Dunbar, to which
allusion was made in the preceding chapter, that John Knox returned to Scotland,
and on the 29th of July, 1567, he preached
a celebrated sermon at the coronation of
James the Sixth, in the church at Stirling.
He also preached on the 15th of December, at the opening of the first parliament
which was held during the minority of
the king, and the regency of the earl of
Murray.   This parliament ratified all the
acts of the year 1560, in favour of the
protestant religion ; enacted new statutes
of the same kind, and neglected nothing
which could contribute to root out the re-

mains of popery, and to establish the reformation.

But while the most part of the nation were in favour of the nobles who had deposed queen Mary, and rejoiced in the just administration of the regent Murray, she had still a party who remained true to her cause, and who only waited a suitable opportunity for again seating her on the throne, and re-establishing the popish religion. Accordingly, on the 2d of May, 1568, the unhappy queen escaped from the castle of Lochleven ; where, as has been already said, she was imprisoned, and was soon joined by numbers of those who were dissatisfied with the state of affairs in the nation. The regent, who was at Glasgow at the time when Mary made her escape, collected what forces he could procure, and marched against her. The two armies met at Langside, in the vicinity of Glasgow ; and although the regent's forces were far inferior to the queen's, he gained a complete victory, and on his side without the loss of many lives. The fate of the queen is very familiar to all who are acquainted with Scottish history. She fled to England, where, for upwards of nineteen years, she was kept a close prisoner by her relative, queen Elisabeth, by whom she was at last, in the most barbarous and unjust manner, put to death by the public executioner.

The queen's party, disappointed by the result of the battle of Langside, resolved to perpetrate a great crime, namely, the assassination of the regent. Several of their first attempts were frustrated ; at last they devised means for effecting their wicked purpose, and a man of the name of Hamilton of Bothwelhaugh, who had been condemned to death, and saved through the clemency of the regent, was the guilty instrument employed to do the wicked deed. This wretch long watched the regent, and at length finding a good opportunity, he shot him through the body on the 23d of January, 1570. Some historians say that Hamilton was actuated to commit this crime by motives of private revenge ; but it is clear that he was blinded by party rage, which drove him to destroy his benefactor.

The regent's death was felt by the nation as an irreparable loss, and the universal sorrow expressed by all ranks showed the high esteem in which he was held. " He was," says an historian, " a man truly good, and worthy to be ranked among the best governors that Scotland ever enjoyed, and therefore to this day he is honoured with the title of the ' good regent.' "

The funeral of the good regent took place on the 14th of February, in the south aisle of St. Giles's church, when Knox preached a sermon on these words : " Blessed are the dead which die in the Lord." While the preacher lamented his death, and feelingly described his virtues, his audience, consisting of upwards of three thousand persons, was dissolved in tears. The grief of the reformer at this mournful event was so great that it proved injurious to his health, and in the month of October he had an apoplectic fit, which for a few days affected his speech. It is almost inconceivable with what joy the report of this, monstrously exaggerated, was circulated by his enemies, both in Scotland and in England. But it pleased God in his holy providence very soon to restore to him the use of speech , and in a few days he was again enabled to pursue his usual duties.

A very unpleasant misunderstanding about the close of this year arose between the reformer and Kirkaldie of Grange, then captain of the castle. One of the soldiers having been committed to prison on a charge of murder, Kirkaldie, with a party from the castle, forced the doors of his confinement in the middle of the night, and rescued the prisoner. On the following Sabbath, Knox, in very severe terms, condemned the conduct of Kirkaldie. Irritated at this circumstance, that officer used very threatening language, which gave rise to suspicions that he might be tempted to offer violence to the person of the reformer. Accordingly the noblemen and gentlemen in Ayrshire wrote to Kirkaldie on the subject, in a manner which shows, at once, the high estimation in which Knox was held, and how valuable they considered his life. " It is difficult for us to believe," said they, " that you should be moved to do any harm to him in whose protection and life, according to our judgment, stands the prosperity and increase of God's church and religion, and so by injuring him to cast down that work which, with so great labours, and manifest dangers, you have helped to build : yet the great interest that we feel in the personage of that man, whom our God has made the first planter, and also the chief waterer of his church among us, moves us to write to you, *protesting that the life and death of our said brother is to us as precious as our own lives and deaths.*"

In March, 1571, several anonymous libels against Knox were affixed to the church doors, accusing him of preaching sedition, by calling the queen an idolater and a friend of murderers. Though the authors of these libels were called upon to come forward, and substantiate their charges, none of them appeared ; but other bills were circulated, threatening to take away his life, if he continued still to give them offence by his speeches. To each of these libels Knox returned an answer from the pulpit, boldly vindicating himself from the false charges thus circulated against him. As to the threatening against his life, he replied, that his life was in His hands who had preserved him from many dangers ; and that he had now arrived at an age at which he could not flee far ; but none could accuse him of having abandoned the people committed to his care, except by their own orders. His enemies then accused him of inconsistency in countenancing the government of England, and of seeking the aid of queen Elizabeth against his native country, notwithstanding he had written against the government of women. This charge Knox also repelled the following Sabbath. After decidedly denying that he ever sought support against his native country, he added, "What I have been to my country, although this unthankful age do not acknowledge, yet the ages to come will be constrained to testify. And thus I cease, requiring of all who have any thing to say against me, to do it as plainly as I discover my actions and sentiments to the world ; for to me it appears most unreasonable that I should, in this my decrepit age, be compelled to fight against shadows and owls, that dare not come to the light."

A reconciliation, it appears, had been in part effected between Knox and Kirkaldie, of whom notice is made before ; for in the month of April, 1571, when the Hamilton faction, who combined against the earl of Lennox, then regent, and threatened the person of Knox, arrived in Edinburgh, and were received into the cattle, Kirkaldie entered into measures to provide for his safety. Still, however, his enemies earnestly desired his destruction ; and his friends were obliged to guard his house during the night lest he should be assassinated. One evening, in particular, a musket ball was fired in at his window with the intention of taking away his life. But He who suffers " no evil to befall" his people disappointed the wicked purpose of the intended murderer ; for Knox had changed his seat that evening to another part of the room, and the ball passed directly over the spot where he had been accustomed to sit, which, had he been in his usual place, would inevitably have proved his death. His friends, alarmed for his safety, earnestly besought him to remove from the city, and to retire to some place of less danger, until the Hamiltons should leave the town. It was not, however, till they informed him of their resolution to defend him even at the hazard of their lives, and that if any of them suffered injury, he would be to blame, that he yielded, though still with great reluctance, to their importunity.

In May, 1571, he visited St. Andrew's, where he remained till August of the following year. During his residence in that city, he was greatly distressed at the miseries to which the nation was subjected by the war between the king's and the queen's adherents. The queen's party having obtained possession of Edinburgh, the protestants suffered every indignity, and their worship was even for a time suspended, while multitudes left the city, and took up their residence chiefly in the town of Leith.

At a meeting of the assembly at Stirling, in August, 1571, he wrote to them a very animated letter, of which the following is a passage : " Because the daily decay of natural strength doth threaten me with a certain and sudden departing from the misery of this life, I exhort you, brethren, yea, in the fear of God, I charge you to take heed to yourselves, and the flock over which God hath placed you ministers. What your behaviour should be, I am not now, nor have I need, as I think, to express ; but to charge you to be faithful, I dare not forget ; and unfaithful you shall be counted before the Lord Jesus, if with your consent, directly or indirectly, you suffer unworthy men to be thrust into the ministry of Christ, under whatever pretence."

The constitution of Knox, which was naturally strong, was now so weakened by his great exertions, that, though he was still able to perform his public duties on the Lord's-day, he could not travel to any distance. He was even obliged to be assisted to walk to the church, and when in the pulpit, he had to rest for some time before he could proceed to preach ; but before he ended his sermon, he was so warmed with his subject, that he forgot his weakness, and spoke with a vigour and eloquence which astonished and delighted his audience. When the assembly met at Perth on the 6th of August, he wrote to them in terms of strong affection and admonition. "Although I have taken my leave," says he, "not only of you, but also of the whole world, and of worldly affairs, I could not, nor cannot cease to admonish you of things which I know to be prejudicial to the church of Jesus Christ, and within the realm. Above all things, *preserve the church from the bondage of universities.* Persuade them to conduct themselves peaceably, and order their schools as Christians ; *but never subject the pulpit to their authority ; neither exempt them from your jurisdic-*

tion. Take heed that nothing proceed
under your name by particular factions.
Do as you will answer before God, who
at present works powerfully, however
blind the world remains ; fight ye in the
truth, and for the liberty of the same ;
and be assured of triumphing with Jesus
Christ, to whose mighty protection I unfeignedly commit you." They returned
an answer approving of his letter, and expressing their ardent wishes for his welfare. He also revised a sermon which
had been preached at Leith by David
Ferguson, minister of Dumferline ; to
which he added his name and the following words : " John Knox, with my dead
hand but glad heart, praising God that
of his mercy he leaves such light to his
church in this desolation."

CHAPTER XI.

James Lawson appointed colleague to Knox—The reformer has a small room fitted up to preach in—His
health continues to decline—Writes to his colleague,
inviting him to come and visit him before he dies—
Shocking " Massacre of St. Bartholomew" in France—
Great distress of the reformer—Declares that God's
judgments will never depart from the house of Guise,
the authors of the butchery—Knox's last sermon and
prayer in the church of the Tolbooth—Striking and affectionate parting between the people and their pastor—
Seized with a violent cough—Death-bed scenes, con-
versations, and anecdotes—His last moments—Expires
without a struggle—His funeral—Eulogy of Knox by the
earl of Morton.

THE civil commotions of the nation
being considerably abated, and the queen's
party having left Edinburgh, the people
who had been obliged to leave that city
returned to their houses. Without any
delay, they sent commissioners to St.
Andrew's, earnestly requesting Knox, if
his health permitted, to return and resume
his labours among them. To this he
agreed, on the express condition, that he
" should not be desired nor pressed in any
sort to cease to speak against the treasonable conduct of those who held out the
castle of Edinburgh, whose treasonable
and tyrannical deeds he would cry out
against as long as he was able to speak ;
and this he requested might be plainly

stated to his brethren, lest they should afterwards repent of the severity against the traitors, or fear to be exposed to danger on his account." The commissioners assured him that he should enjoy the same freedom of speech, and that they wished him to discharge his duties in the same manner as he had formerly done.

During the absence of Knox from Edinburgh, a difference had taken place between his colleague Craig and the congregation ; in consequence of which, they agreed to separate. With the advice of Knox, they chose James Lawson, a man of great learning and piety, to supply his place.

The reformer arrived in Edinburgh about the latter end of August, and on the Sunday succeeding, he preached in the church of St. Giles, to the great satisfaction of the inhabitants ; but his voice having become so feeble, that the congregation could not distinctly hear him, he desired a smaller house to be provided, where he could be heard, though it were only by a hundred people. This request was readily complied with, and a suitable place was immediately fitted up.

But the health of the reformer was

daily and visibly declining ; and being
now quite unable to perform the duties of
his office, he sent the following letter with
the commissioners to his new colleague
Lawson, urging him not to delay a moment in coming to Edinburgh :—" All
worldly strength," he writes, " yea, even
in things spiritual, decays, and yet shall
never the work of God decay.   Beloved
brother, seeing that God of his mercy, far
beyond my expectation, hath called me
once again to Edinburgh, and yet that I
feel nature so decayed, and daily decay-
ing, that I look not for a long continuance
of my battle, I would gladly once discharge my conscience into your bosom,
and into the bosom of others, in whom I
think the fear of God remains.   If I had
ability of body, I should not now put you
to the trouble which I now require of
you ; that is, once to visit me, that we may
confer together of heavenly things ; for in
earth there is no stability, except ever
fighting under the cross of the Lord Jesus
Christ, to whose mighty protection I
heartily commit you.—Make haste, my
brother, else you will come too late."

The infirmities of Knox were now
rapidly increasing ; but the melancholy

tidings of the horrid massacre of the protestants at Paris, and of the murder of the
good admiral Coligni, the great supporter
of the protestant cause in France, inflicted
the severest wound on his already en-
feebled frame, and saddened the remain-
ing days of his life.

This dreadful event is known in the
history of France by the name of the
" Massacre of St. Bartholomew."   In the
course of a single week, besides the admiral, a number of other distinguished cha-
racters, with twelve hundred gentlemen,
and about one hundred thousand protestants in Paris, and other parts of France,
were cruelly butchered ; and for some
days the streets of Paris literally ran with
blood.   This   inhuman   massacre   (for
which the pope of Rome held a jubilee !)
was begun on St. Bartholomew's day,
August 24th, 1572, and while the friends
of the reformation in England and Scotland mourned over the sufferings of their
brethren, they were justly alarmed at the
blow which they perceived was levelled
against the whole protestant body.   But
Divine justice soon overtook the principal
contrivers of this horrid work of destruction.

Knox publicly inveighed against the treacherous cruelty of the king of France, and scrupled not to declare, that " sentence was denounced in Scotland against that murderer ; that God's judgments would never depart from his house ; but that his name should remain an execration to posterity, while none of his descendants should enjoy the kingdom in peace and quietness, unless repentance prevented God's judgments." The French ambassador, Le Croc, highly offended at Knox, desired the regent to prohibit him from thus declaiming against his master. But the regent, at once, declined interfering in the matter.

Lawson arrived in Edinburgh about the middle of September, and preached a sermon, to the very great satisfaction of the people. This was on Friday, and on the next Sabbath Knox began to preach in the Tolbooth church, which he continued to do as long as his health permitted. On the 9th of November, he admitted Lawson as his colleague and successor in the large church, after he had preached in the Tolbooth, when he proposed the usual questions, explained the mutual duties of a minister and his people, and prayed that any gifts which had been conferred on himself might be increased on his successor a thousand fold. On no previous occasion did he speak with greater power. He called God to witness that he had walked with a good conscience before them, not studying to please men, or to serve his own affections, but in all sincerity and truth, preaching to them the gospel of Christ. He exhorted them to stand fast in the faith which they had professed ; and having fervently prayed for the continuance of God's blessing upon them, he took his last farewell. He was assisted home, and as he passed along, the people, who had lined the high street from the church to his house, took a final and affectionate view of their beloved pastor.

Two days after these events, he was seized with a violent cough, which so afflicted him as to oblige him to give up his ordinary practice of reading every day some chapters of the Old and New Testaments, with a portion of the Psalms, the whole of which he used to peruse once a month. But he requested his wife and Richard Bannatyne, his servant (or rather his secretary), to read to him every day the 17th chapter of John ; a chapter of the

Epistle to the Ephesians ; and the 53d chapter of Isaiah ; to which order they attended with the strictest punctuality. Sometimes also sermons were read to him, and when his attendants, thinking him to be asleep, would ask him if he heard what they read, he would answer, " I hear, I praise God, and I understand far better." When his friends proposed to call a physician he consented, saying that he would not either neglect or despise ordinary means, though he was persuaded that the Lord would shortly put an end to his sufferings. On the 13th, he ordered his servants to be paid their wages, and at the same time exhorted them to walk in the fear of the Lord, as became Christians who had been educated in his family.

On Friday the 14th he rose about seven o'clock, though he was scarcely able to sit up, imagining it was the Lord's-day. When asked why he had risen, he replied, that he had been meditating during the night on the resurrection of Christ, and that he meant to go to church to preach on that consoling doctrine to his people. How ardent was the desire of this good man, even in his last moments, to engage in the service of his Master, though he was so weak in body that he had to be supported by two men from his bedside!

Being anxious to meet once more with the members of his church, he sent for his colleague, Dawson, and several other individuals ; and addressed them in words of the following import :—" The time is approaching for which I have so often longed, when I shall be relieved from all my cares, and be with my Saviour, Christ, for ever. And now God is my witness, whom I have served with my spirit in the gospel of his Son, that I have taught nothing but true and sound doctrine, and that the end I proposed in all my preaching was to instruct the ignorant, to confirm the weak, to raise up and comfort with the promises of God's mercies the troubled consciences of those who were humbled under a sense of sin, and to beat down by the threatening of God's judgments the stubborn and the proud. I am not ignorant that many have blamed me for my undue severity, but God knows that I never in my heart hated those whom I censured. I indeed hated their sins, and every thing in them that was contrary to God ; and I laboured to win them to Christ. My impartiality in reproving men of every rank was dic-

tated by the fear of God, who judges without respect of persons, who placed me in
the ministry, and who will call me to account. I feared not the faces of men
(weak, unworthy, and fearful as in myself
I am), because this fear of the Lord was
before my eyes. And now, brethren,
stand fast in the doctrine which ye have
been taught ; look diligently to the flocks
with whose oversight God hath intrusted
you, and which he hath redeemed to himself by the blood of his only begotten
Son ; join not with the ungodly ; guard
against connecting yourselves with the
faction who wish to restore the queen ;
and rather choose with David to flee to
mountains, than remain in the company of
the wicked, whom, except they repent,
God will assuredly destroy both in body
and spirit. And do you, my brother Lawson, fight the good fight, do the work of the
Lord with courage, and with a willing
mind, and God from above bless you and
the church of which you have the oversight ; believing that against it, as long as
it holds fast the doctrine of truth, even the
gates of hell shall never prevail."

Knox was completely exhausted with
speaking so long ; and, having prayed

fervently for the Divine blessing upon them, and the increase of the Spirit upon their new pastor, they took an affectionate leave of him, weeping, and in the deepest affliction. Before going away, he privately requested his colleague and Lindsay to carry a message to the laird of Grange, who held out the castle against the party that was attached to the king. "There is one thing," said he, "that grieveth me exceedingly; you have formerly seen the courage and constancy of the laird of Grange ; and now, unhappy man, he hath cast himself away. I pray you go to him, and tell him from me, that unless he forsake his present course of wicked conduct, neither that rock (meaning the castle) on which he confides, nor the carnal wisdom of that man (meaning Maitland) whom he counts half a god, shall preserve him ; but he shall be shamefully pulled out of his nest, and hung before the sun, except he be granted repentance. That man's soul is dear to me, and I would earnestly have him to be saved." The two ministers complied with his request, and delivered Knox's message to the governor. At first he appeared somewhat moved, but on consulting with Maitland he returned a very haughty answer. This being reported to Knox, he was exceedingly distressed, and said he had been earnest in prayer to God for him, and still hoped, though he should die a shameful death, that his soul would be saved. The following year the castle was forced to surrender, and the governor was condemned to be executed. On the scaffold he desired Lindsay to repeat the words of Knox, and seemed to take comfort from the hope that the latter part of the wish would be granted.

On Wednesday the 19th, several noblemen visited him, among whom was the earl of Morton, whom he addressed in the following language. " God has given you many blessings ; he has given you wisdom, riches, many great and good friends ; and is now to prefer you to the government of this realm. In his name, then, I charge you that you use these blessings aright, and better in time to come than you have done in times past. In all your actions seek first the glory of God, the furtherance of the gospel, the maintenance of his church and ministry ; and next, be careful of the king, to procure his good, and the welfare of the realm. If you do this, God will be with you and honour you ; but if you do otherwise, he shall deprive you of all these blessings, and your end shall be shame and ignominy." These words, an historian observes, were remembered by the earl of Morton nine years afterwards at the time of his execution, when he acknowledged that he found them by experience to be true.

A religious lady, desiring him to praise God for the good he had done, and beginning to speak of his usefulness, he interrupted her by saying, " Lady, flesh of itself is too proud, and needs no incitement to self-conceit." He exhorted her to lay aside pride, and be clothed with humility ; and declared that as for himself he relied solely on the free mercy of God, manifested to men through Christ Jesus, whom he embraced as his wisdom, righteousness, sanctification, and redemption. All who were present having left him except the laird of Braid, Knox said to him, " Every one bids me good-night but yourself ; I have been greatly indebted to you, for which I shall never be able to recompense you ; but I commit you to one who is able to do it, that is, to the eternal God."

On Friday the 21st, he desired Richard Bannatyne to order his coffin to be made. He was that day much engaged in prayer, often saying, "Come, Lord Jesus ! into thy hands I commend my spirit. Look in mercy on thy church which thou hast redeemed, and restore peace to this afflicted commonwealth. Raise up pastors after thine own heart, who will take care of thy church ; and grant that we may learn, as well from the blessings as from the chastisements of thy providence, to abhor sin, and love thee with full purpose of heart." Then addressing those around him, he said, "O wait on the Lord with fear, and death will not be terrible ; yea, blessed and holy will their death be who are interested in the death of the Son of God." Being asked if he suffered much pain, he replied, "I cannot look upon that as pain which will soon prove the end of all mortality and trouble, and the beginning of eternal life."

During the time of the afternoon sermon of Sabbath the 23d, after having lain a long time quiet, he suddenly exclaimed, "If any be present, let them come and see the work of God." Shortly afterwards he said, "I have been for two nights meditating on the troubled state of the church of God, the spouse of Jesus Christ, despised by the world, but precious in his sight. I have called on God for her, and committed her to Christ her head. I have been fighting against Satan, who is ever ready to assault ; yea, I have fought against spiritual wickedness in heavenly things, and have prevailed. I have been, as it were, in heaven, and tasted of the heavenly joys." He then repeated the Lord's prayer and the creed, making some remarks on each petition and article ; adding, when repeating, "' Our Father which art in heaven'— Who can pronounce such holy words ?" After sermon he was visited by numbers. some of whom, when they saw him so exhausted, asked him if he felt great pain. To this he replied, " I have no more pain than he who is already in heaven, and would be contented to lie here seven years, if such were the will of God." He was often engaged in meditation and prayer, when those around him thought he was asleep ; sometimes saying, " Live in Christ : Lord grant us a just and perfect hatred of sin : Lord give true pastors to thy church, that purity of doctrine may be continued, and restore peace to the nation, with goodly rulers and magistrates." Afterwards, lifting up his hands to heaven, he cried out, " To thee, O Lord, do I commit myself. Thou knowest how intense my pains are : but I do not complain : yea, Lord, if such be thy will concerning me, I would be content to bear these pains for many years together; only do thou continue to enlighten my mind through Christ Jesus." Once he exclaimed, " Lord, make an end of trouble : Lord, I commend my soul, body and all, into thy hands."

On Monday, the 24th, which was the last day of his life, he rose between nine and ten o'clock, and, though he was unable to stand alone, put on part of his clothes. After sitting in his chair about half an hour, he went to bed again. Being asked if he had much pain : he said, " It is no painful pain, but such as, I trust, will put an end to my warfare. I must leave the care of my wife and children to you, to whom you must be a husband in my room."

In the afternoon he desired his wife to read the 15th chapter of First Corinthians, which being done, he said, " Is not that a comfortable chapter ?" Shortly after, lifting up his head and pointing to heaven, he said, " Now, for the last time, I commend my soul, body, and spirit into thy hand, O Lord!" About five o'clock he said to his wife, " Go, read where I cast my first anchor ;" when she read the seventeenth chapter of John, and afterwards some sermons. Having spent some time in great apparent uneasiness, Dr. Preston asked him, after he awaked, what made him moan and sigh so heavily in his sleep. " I have been often tempted," replied he, " by Satan to despair, but he could not prevail. Now he has tempted me to trust in myself, and to rejoice and glory in my labours, as if I should merit heaven by the faithful discharge of my duties. But I have expelled him with these passages of Scripture, ' What hast thou that thou hast not received ?' ' Not I, but the grace of God in me.' ' By the grace of God I am what I am.' Therefore, I give thanks to God who has given me the victory ; and now I am sure that, without pain of body, or distress of mind I shall soon close this mortal and miserable life, for that happy and immortal life which shall never have an end."

Family worship was performed about half-past ten, which being finished, Dr. Preston asked him if he had heard the prayers ; when he emphatically replied, *" Would to God that you and all men heard them as I have done !* I praise God for that heavenly sound." A little afterwards he gave a deep sigh, and said, *" Now it is come. "* Richard Bannatyne then addressed him in these words : "Now, sir, the time for which you have long called to God is come, and seeing that all natural powers fail, recollect those comfortable promises which you have often shown to us of our Saviour, Jesus Christ : and that we may know that you hear us, give us some sign." Upon this he lifted up his hand, and sighing twice, expired without a struggle. *Surely the latter end of the righteous is peace !* " In this manner," says Bannatyne, " departed this man of God, the light of Scotland, the comfort of the church, the pattern and example of all true ministers, in purity of life, soundness of doctrine, and boldness in reproving of wickedness ; one that cared not for the favour of men, how great soever they were, but faithfully reproved all their abuses and sins."

He was buried in the churchyard at St.
Giles, on Wednesday, the 26th of November.   His funeral was attended by the
earl of Morton, newly elected regent, by
the other lords who were in the city, and
by a vast number of people, who deeply
lamented his death as a great national calamity.   When laid in the grave, the earl
of Morton, though often the object of his
censure, did justice to his character in
these words :   " There lies he who never
feared the face of man ; who hath often
been threatened with pistol and dagger ;
but yet hath ended his days in peace and
honour ; for Providence watched over him
in a special manner, when his very life
was in danger."

CHAPTER XII.

Description of the reformer's person—The family he left
behind—Interesting anecdote of Mrs. Welch, one of his
daughters—The character of the reformer misrepresented
by popish writers—His true character—Distinction to be
drawn between the *man* and the *reformer.*

JOHN KNOX was a man of small stature,
and of a weakly constitution ; and, according to the custom of the times, wore a long
beard reaching down to his middle.   He
left behind him a widow and five children,
two sons, and three daughters.   Nathaniel,
the eldest of his sons, died in the year
1580, and Eleazer, the youngest, in 1591 ;
none of them leaving any posterity.   One
of his daughters was married to Robert
Pont, minister of St. Cuthbert's ; another
of them to James Fleming, also a minister
of the church of Scotland ; and Elisabeth,
the third daughter, to John Welch, minister of Ayr.

The following anecdote of Mrs. Welch,
daughter of the reformer, forms an illus-
tration of that period, and would seem to
show that she had inherited no small portion of her father's fearlessness.   Her husband was sentenced to death for resistance
to some measures of James the Sixth ; but

his sentence being changed into banishment, he went to France accompanied by his wife, where after a long residence he lost his health.   His physicians informing him that the only prospect he had of recovering was by returning to his native country, he went to London.   King James, however, absolutely refused to permit him to return to Scotland ; upon which Mrs. Welch found means of obtaining access to the king, and petitioned him to grant her husband this liberty.   The king asked her how many children her father had left, and if they were boys or girls ?   She said, three, and they were all girls.   " I am thankful," exclaimed the king, " for if they had been three lads, I had never enjoyed my three kingdoms in peace."   At last he told her, that if she would persuade her husband to submit to his wishes, he would suffer him to return to Scotland ; when Mrs. Welch, knowing the import of these conditions, lifted her apron, and holding it towards the king, replied, in the spirit of her father, " Please your majesty, I would rather receive his head in this apron."

No man has been more traduced by popish writers than Knox ; but " wisdom

is justified of her children." His character requires no vindication. His life, from
first to last, is an enduring memorial of
his learning and ability ; the purity of his
motives in all his transactions—his disinterestedness and zeal in the service of
God, and for the good of his country—his
intrepidity in difficulty or danger—his
faithfulness in reproving vice, and en-
couraging holiness—and the piety which
marked his character, both in public and
in private ;—all which prove better than
any defence which might here be attempted, that the charges of his enemies
are as unfounded as they are unjust. He
was, indeed, austere, stern, and vehement ;
often averse to moderation, and liberal of
his censures, without respect of persons.
Yet these very characteristics, for which
he has been blamed, were absolutely necessary for constituting him a reformer in
the rude age in which he lived. Had he
been of a mild and more gentle spirit, he
would have been totally unfit for the office
to which he was called. An eminent
historian, Dr. Robertson, thus describes
his character. " Zeal, intrepidity, and
disinterestedness were virtues which he
possessed in an eminent degree. Rigid

and uncomplying himself, he showed no indulgence to the infirmities of others. Regardless of the distinctions of rank and character, he uttered his admonitions with an acrimony and vehemence more apt to irritate than to reclaim. Those very qualities, however, which now render his character less amiable, fitted him to be the instrument of Providence for advancing the reformation among a fierce people, and enabling him to face dangers, and to surmount opposition, from which a person of a more gentle spirit would have been apt to shrink back. By an unwearied application to study and to business, as well as by the frequency and fervour of his public discourses, he had worn out a constitution naturally robust."

Smeaton, one of his contemporaries, gives him the following character : " I know not if ever God placed a more godly and great spirit in so weak and frail a body. I am certain there can scarcely be found another in whom the gifts of the Holy Ghost shone so bright to the comfort of the church in Scotland. No one spared himself less ; no one was more diligent in the charge committed to him; and yet no man was more the object of the

wicked's hatred, or more frequently as-
saulted with the reproach of evil speakers.
But this was so far from abating, that it
rather strengthened his courage and resolution in the ways of God."

But indeed it may be said there was no
point of duty in which Knox did not shine
with uncommon lustre. The duties of
the ministry were discharged by him with
the greatest assiduity, fidelity, and fervour ; and no circumstances prevented
him from appearing in the pulpit. The
letters he wrote to his friends breathe a
spirit of the most ardent piety. The religious meditations in which he spent his
last sickness were not confined to that
period of his life ; they had been his ha-
bitual employment from the time that he
was brought to the knowledge of the truth,
and his solace amidst the hardships and
perils through which he had passed. With
his brethren in the ministry he lived in
the utmost cordiality. We never read of
the slightest variance between him and
any of his colleagues. While he was
dreaded and hated by the licentious and
profane, whose vices he never spared, the
religious and sober part of his countrymen
felt a veneration for him, which was

founded on his unblemished reputation,
as well as his popular talents as a preacher.
In private life he was both beloved and
revered by his friends and domestics.

The fact is, that in contemplating such
a character as that of Knox, it is not the
man so much as *the reformer* that ought
to engage our attention.   The talents
which are suited to one age and station
would be altogether unsuitable to another :
and the wisdom displayed by Providence
in raising up persons endowed with qualities singularly adapted to the work which
they have to perform for the benefit of
mankind, demands our particular consideration.   To those who complain that
they are disappointed at not finding in
the reformer courteous manners and a
winning address, it may be replied, in the
language of our Lord to the Jews, concerning John the Baptist, "What went ye out
into the wilderness for to see ?   A reed
shaken with the wind ?   What went ye
out for to see ?   A man clothed in soft
raiment ?   Behold they which are gor-
geously apparelled, and live delicately, are
in king's courts. But what went ye out for
to see ?   A prophet ? yea, I say unto you,
and more than a prophet !"

CHAPTER XIII.

The character of the great reformer better understood
since the publication of Dr. McCrie's " Life of Knox"—
Description of the superb monument erected to the
reformer—Various ceremonies and solemnities which accompanied its establishment—The procession—The sermon—The prayer—Inscription on the monument—End.

In this chapter, which is the last, it is
proper to give some short notices of the
splendid monument erected in Glasgow
to the great " Scottish reformer," an en-
graving of which accompanies this little
volume.   The people of Scotland, it is
observed, were very tardy in doing
justice to the memory of their great
benefactor.   Indeed, his character was
not properly appreciated till the appearance of Dr. McCrie's celebrated "Life of
Knox," before which he had suffered
greatly from the false representations of
hostile writers.   After the publication of
Dr. McCrie's book, the current of public
opinion became changed in favour of the
reformer, and people began to talk of
some public testimony of respect.   " But
this," says McGavin, " would probably
have terminated in mere talk, but for the
well-directed zeal of the Reverend Dr.
McGill, professor of divinity in the university of Glasgow.   He was the first to

bring the subject before the public, and by most persevering activity, aided by the good offices of some of the most influential citizens, and of many friends to the cause at a distance, a sufficient sum was raised for erecting the column and statue to the north of the city of Glasgow."*

That the erection of the first monument in Scotland to the memory of its great reformer should be held in remembrance, it was deemed advisable to lay the foundation stone with due solemnity, in presence of the subscribers, and that the Rev. Dr. McGill, the pious, learned, and intrepid defender of the principles of the reformation, and the projector of the monument, should be requested to lay the foundation stone ; and, farther, that the celebrated Dr. Chalmers should be requested to preach a sermon on the occasion, and the venerable Dr. Burns to offer up prayers for the success of the undertaking : all which was duly performed.

On Thursday, the 22d of September, 1825, the immense procession formed, and moved towards the church, which was crowded to excess. The Rev. Dr. Chal-

* See Life of John Knox, by Wm. McGavin, prefixed to Knox's Hist of the Reform. in Scotland. Glasgow, 1831.

mers preached from Jeremiah vi. 16.—
" Thus saith the Lord, stand ye in the
ways, and see, and ask for the old paths,
where is the good way, and walk therein,
and ye shall find rest for your souls." After the sermon was finished, a collection
was raised in aid of the subscription fund.

When divine service was ended, the
procession formed again and began to
move.   The interest shown at this cere-
monial was of the deepest kind.   The
streets through which the procession
passed were so crowded, that it was with
difficulty they moved along.   The win-
dows and housetops were all overcrowded
with spectators.   When they approached
the place of destination, the scene was
truly magnificent, when in looking down
the churchyard, in front of the cathedral,
the eye beheld probably ten thousand persons, whose continued shouts of approbation rent the air.

As soon as this dense mass arrived at
the site of the monument, silence was
proclaimed, and from a lofty scaffold
erected for the purpose, Dr. Burns offered
up a suitable and impressive prayer, which
concluded in these words :—" And now,
Lord, we pray for a blessing on our pre-

sent undertaking, in erecting an honourable monument to the memory of our
great reformer, John Knox ; a man raised
up by Thee, and endowed with those qualities which peculiarly fitted him for being
a distinguished instrument in the arduous
work of delivering this nation from spiritual thraldom and civil tyranny.   Every
time that we and our posterity look to
this patriotic monument, may our hearts
rise in gratitude to Thee for the blessings
we enjoy.   May we be sensible of our
inestimable privileges, both civil and sacred, and carefully improve them.   May
our liberty never degenerate into licen-
tiousness, nor our gratitude abate ; but
may we be as eminent for the holiness
of our lives as we are distinguished by
our national blessings.   Hear these our
prayers, for the sake of Jesus Christ our
Lord, and to thy name be the praise now
and for evermore.   Amen."

At the conclusion of the prayer, several ceremonies, usual on such occasions,
were performed.   These ceremonies over,
Mr. Cleland, a member of the committee of
management, read aloud the inscription,
which was on a metal plate.   The monument has four inscriptions—one on the

west side, one on the south, and one on the east, all which have more or less reference to the reformation ; but the one on the north side of the monument most particularly relates to Knox ; and is as follows—

To testify gratitude for inestimable services
in the cause of Religion, Education, and Civil Liberty ;
to awaken admiration
of that integrity, disinterestedness, and courage,
which stood unshaken in the midst of trials,
and in the maintenance of the highest objects ;
Finally,
To cherish unceasing reverence for the principles and
blessings of that great Reformation,
by the influence of which our country, through the
midst of difficulties,
has risen to honour, prosperity, and happiness,
This monument is erected by voluntary contribution.
To the memory of
JOHN KNOX,
The chief instrument, under God,
of the Reformation of Scotland,
on the xxi. day of September, MDCCCXXV.
He died, rejoicing in the faith of the gospel,
At Edinburgh, on the xxiv. of November, A. D. MDLXXII
in the sixty-seventh year of his age

THE END.

From Wilderness Pioneer to the Oval Office

Born to his widowed mother just months after his father's death, as a young teenager, **Andrew Jackson** was cruelly treated by the British as a prisoner of war, losing two brothers and his mother during the American Revolution. Though he did not become the minister his mother hoped he would be, he became a popular hero and America's seventh president. Jackson's legacy is a controversial one due to his support for slavery and forced removal of Native Americans from their lands. Exemplifying the rough and hardy qualities of a frontiersman, Jackson would see success on the battlefield, including the brilliant campaign against the British in New Orleans during the War of 1812, survive an attempted assassination as president, and fiercely resist the institution of a national bank.

5 x 7 • 400 pages • Case Bound
Retail: $19.99
Release Date: February 2011
ISBN 13: 978-0-89051-603-4

Available where fine books are sold or go to www.nlpg.com.

A Controversial Leader and Visionary Man of God!

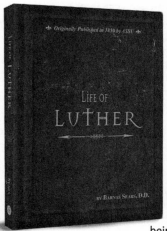

Martin Luther is one of early Christianity's most pivotal figures, and now in this detailed biography reproduced from an 1850 American Sunday School Union original, you can learn more about this influential and enigmatic man. From his early years, to his religious education, to the events leading up to the Protestant Reformation, you will discover the views and experiences that led to his excommunication by the Pope in 1520. The book recounts detailed correspondence and accounts that shed further light on Luther's dispute with the Catholic Church over indulgences being purchased to avoid punishment from sin and why he chose to defiantly translate the Bible from Latin to the language of the common man so they could read the biblical truth for themselves.

The book is a comprehensive presentation of Martin Luther's life and contributions to the faith that impact our lives even today. Often controversial, sometimes visionary, and defiantly confident of his actions, the *Life of Luther* is a fascinating and important historical account you won't want to miss!

5 x 7 • 496 pages • Case Bound
Retail: $17.99
ISBN 13: 978-0-89051-599-0

The Faith of Our First Founding Father!

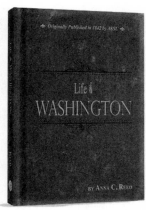

As modern revisionists seek to minimize or erase all traces of America's Christian heritage, a very rare vintage biography sheds a remarkable light of truth on the life of our first president, **George Washington**!

Originally published by the American Sunday School Union (ASSU), *The Life of Washington* is a fascinating read.

Anna C. Reed, the niece of a signer of the Declaration of Independence, authored this amazing work for ASSU prior to 1850. Originally translated into over 20 languages within a few years, the book was among the most widely-read biographies of Washington at the time.

For over two hundred years, the American Sunday School Union provided quality books and Christian education titles for young people through their missions to start Sunday School programs, and eventually began church planting, church camps, and numerous other programs. ASSU missionaries carried books in saddlebags to leave with these fledgling schools, promoting literacy, education, and the very best in Christan moral values.

5 x 7 • 290 pages • Case Bound
Retail: $16.99
ISBN 13: 978-0-89051-578-5